"Messianic anticipation begins builds in the rest of the Old Tes the birth of the Lord Jesus Chris William Varner shows us that th.. .... of our Lord were rooted in the Messianic hope of the Old Testament. This is both powerful and spiritually enriching."

John MacArthur
Pastor, Grace Community Church

"From the first chapter ("Holy Heartburn") to the last ("Will the Real Messiah Please Stand Up?"), Will Varner's book will grip your mind and stir your heart as you read about Jesus, God's Messiah for His people. Each chapter is filled with Scriptural truth and amazing spiritual insight into texts we have been reading our whole lives. Fair warning – if you start the book, you won't be able to put it down until you have turned the final page! And when you are finished, you will long even more for Messiah to come again!"

Sam Horn
President, The Master's University and Seminary

"You will be fully satisfied as you digest Dr. Varner's work that employs the unique blend of Jewish historical and cultural backgrounds, careful Scriptural exegesis, and thoughtful insights coming from years of immersive study that weaves together the unfolding prophetic message of the advent of Jesus the Messiah."

Steve Pettit
President, Bob Jones University

ANTICIPATING THE ADVENT

ANTICIPATING THE ADVENT

Looking for Messiah in All the Right Places

WILLIAM VARNER

Fontes Press

Anticipating the Advent:
Looking for Messiah in All the Right Places

Copyright © 2020 by William Varner

ISBN-13: 978-1-948048-45-3 (hardback)
ISBN-13: 978-1-948048-46-0 (paperback)

Prayer icons at the end of each chapter are made by Freepik from www.flaticon.com.

FONTES PRESS

DALLAS, TX

www.fontespress.com

This book is dedicated to

Gary Cohen and Marvin Rosenthal

Two Jewish followers of the Messiah

who have greatly influenced my ministry

Contents

Foreword

Growing up in an observant Jewish home, my family did not really deal with Christmas that much. Our encounters were predominantly seeing the lights strung on our neighbors' homes and across the boulevard in our neighborhood. My Hebrew School teachers explained that Christmas was derived from pagan roots, but the Christmas songs I heard playing in the mall and on the radio didn't seem to fit. There was *O Little Town of Bethlehem*, about a village in Israel, the hometown of David Ha-Melech, the Jewish King David. I heard the refrain from *The First Noel*, "Born is the King of Israel." One song seemed to anticipate King Messiah who would "ransom captive Israel." This was all so intriguing to me, that I watched the original airing of *A Charlie Brown Christmas*, hearing the Lukan Christmas story for the first time from the lips of Linus. In fact, those were the very first words I'd ever heard from the New Testament. And I was hooked—more and more I wanted to know about this festival that could transform Ebenezer Scrooge from miser to benefactor. It could even create good will among Gentile storekeepers and neighbors that were usually grouchy with each other and with us, the Jewish people in the neighborhood.

Then, as a freshman in high school, as part of a story that is too long and complicated to be mentioned here, I began to study the messianic passages of the Hebrew Bible. Before too long, by spring, I became a follower of Jesus. In a sense, I realized that the star that led the magi and shone over the manger in Bethlehem was actually a star of David! Celebrating the birth of the Jewish Messiah Jesus was truly the most Jewish of festivals. The following December, I determined to celebrate *Messiahmas* in a way that reflected my Jewish identity. I began to study the messianic passages about Messiah's birth. Most importantly, I wanted to understand the biblical and theological aspects revealed in Scripture regarding the birth of the divine Son of God. To be blunt, I did not have one resource that could help me with all that, though I longed for one.

Now so many years later, my friend Will Varner has produced the book I looked for so long ago. This book, *Anticipating the Advent*, gives us just what we need, with a deep and biblical perspective. Will has provided expositions of the messianic passages about Messiah's advent, illuminated the historical setting and described the world to which Messiah came, and clarified the biblical and theological implications of God breaking into human history through the birth of the Messiah Yeshua. Along the way, Will also provides spiritual insights to renew our appreciation of the story of the birth of the King.

Anticipating the Advent will enable us to recapture our love for celebrating the birth of Messiah by rooting it firmly in the soil of Scripture, not in the world of Dickens. It will refresh and renew us by helping us to come and adore Him, the King of Israel and the world, in a deeper and more meaningful way. So, sit back, dig in, and learn from this master teacher the biblical truths surrounding the birth of Jesus the Messiah.

Michael Rydelnik
Professor of Jewish Studies and Bible, Moody Bible Institute; Host and Teacher, *Open Line with Dr. Michael Rydelnik*, Moody Radio

Preface

For over thirty years I have taught a course titled "The Life of the Messiah" to students from all backgrounds. Another course that I have often taught is titled "Messianic Theology." I was also privileged to publish a book titled *The Messiah: Revealed, Rejected, and Received.* Thus the teaching that Jesus of Nazareth was the Messiah of Israel has dominated my life for decades! In the Spring of 2020, I was privileged to focus attention again on the Messianic role of Jesus in the last days of his earthly life in the book *Passionate about the Passion Week* (Fontes Press). A dear friend reminded me that since I focused that last book on the Passion Week and beyond, I should now turn my attention to the Advent themes. I have been able to draw upon some earlier writings and revise them and update them for this book. A number of new chapters also appear here for the first time. Each of them has grown out of my preaching and teaching about the coming of the Messiah into this world. As I did in my *Passion* book, I suggest a fresh look at a number of old themes, but His "Advent," however, included more than His birth. Therefore, I have also looked at some subsequent events in the Messiah's life and ministry. If a reader thinks that I have omitted such great passages as Psalm 22 and Isaiah 53, I would encourage them to see what I have written about His sacrificial death and resurrection in that earlier volume.

This is not a long book and I encourage readers to consider using it around your Advent/Christmas/Nativity celebrations. Also if this book finds itself in the hands of my Jewish friends, I hope that you will give it an attentive read. This Jewish Messiah changed the life of this Gentile boy over fifty years ago, and I just cannot stop writing about Him! G. K. Chesterton wrote that the purpose of an open mind is the same as the purpose of an open mouth—to eventually close on something that is satisfying. My prayer is that the readers of this volume will approach it with an open mind that will eventually close on something that fully satisfies their effort.

The Scripture quotations are my own translations, influenced by the ESV and NASB versions, unless otherwise noted. I have also added a suggested prayer at the end of each chapter, each uniquely adapted from a prayer in the Bible. For years I have been blessed by learning to pray Scripture back to God. It is my prayer that your own prayer response to these chapters will echo the thoughts in these inspired and inspiring Scriptural praises and petitions! I believe it is important to see these studies on the person of the Messiah as a spiritual exercise and not just as an intellectual effort.

CHAPTER 1

A Holy Heartburn

The passengers were seated in the jetliner as it climbed to its cruising altitude. Over the intercom came a calm voice notifying everyone that the plane was fully automated—in fact, there were no cabin attendants on board and not even any pilots! This miracle of science, the voice continued, was thoroughly dependable because all mechanisms were fail-safe. To further assist the listeners, the taped voice of the plane's computer went on to say, "There is no need to fear, because nothing can possibly go wrong . . . go wrong . . . go wrong . . . go . . ."

Have you ever had an experience in which you thought everything would work out perfectly, only to find your plans come crashing down through an unexpected and disappointing turn of events? This was the personal experience of Cleopas and his unnamed friend as they trudged heavily toward a village called Emmaus seven miles west of Jerusalem one spring Sunday afternoon in the year AD 30. Their story is recounted for us in Luke 24:13–35. What was the reason for their discouragement? How did the stranger who joined their walk minister to their despondency? The answers to these questions offer insights into the attitudes of Jewish people, past and present, about the Messiah. Such answers also provide valuable instructions to all who want to better understand God's program of redemption for mankind.

Luke tells us that these two disciples were discussing the meaning of the tragic events that had transpired over the previous week. As they conversed, Jesus joined them on the road, but they failed to recognize Him. Jesus then inquired about the reason for their sad countenances and morbid conversation. Surprised that He appeared unaware of the recent events, they quickly summarized them for Him:

> And He said to them, "What things?" And they said to Him, "Concerning Jesus of Nazareth, a man who was a prophet mighty in deed and word before God and all the people, and how our chief priests and rulers delivered Him up to be condemned to death, and crucified Him. But we had hoped that He was the one to redeem Israel. Yes, and besides all this, it is now the third day since these things happened. Moreover, some women of our company amazed us. They were at the tomb early in the morning, and when they did not find His body, they came back saying that they had even seen a vision of angels, who said that He was alive. Some of those who were with us went to the tomb and found it just as the women had said, but Him they did not see!" (Luke 24:19–24).

Solomon reminds us that "Hope deferred makes the heart sick . . ." (Prov 13:12a). If ever there were living examples of that proverb, it was this discouraged, despondent and heartsick pair! Their fervent hopes for Messianic freedom had been dashed to pieces. Everything that seemed to have been going so well had fallen apart in a few short days. Like so many Jews of their age, they had longed for a Messiah. In their eyes this Son of David would break the despised Roman yoke of oppression and lead tiny Judea into the freedom it had not experienced since the glory days of the Maccabees over one hundred years earlier. Therefore, when Jesus had appeared, performing wonders and proclaiming a

"Kingdom," their hearts burned with the hopes of a new David so that His Jewish subjects would live under their own rule, not that of the Gentiles. They had become distraught at this unexpected turn of events, even to the point of discounting the reports from some women that Jesus actually had returned from the dead. In light of this tragic set of circumstances, they had decided to return home to Emmaus and to begin picking up the shattered pieces of their lives.

Having listened patiently to their disheartened report, Jesus then began to minister to their hearts in a very direct way. It cannot be emphasized too much the absolutely vital importance of the words with which He challenged them.

> And He said to them, "O foolish ones, and slow of heart to believe all that the prophets have spoken! Was it not necessary for the Messiah to suffer these things and to enter into His glory?" Then beginning with Moses and with all the prophets, He explained to them the things concerning Himself in all the Scriptures (Luke 24:25–27).

In these words are found (1) the answer to the problem of the two disciples and (2) the answer to one of the chief Jewish objections to the Messianic claims of Jesus of Nazareth. Those two discouraged disciples had considered Jesus' rejection and suffering as incompatible with their own view of Messiah as a conquering deliverer of the Jewish people. For nearly two thousand years, many rabbis have sought to discount the claim that Jesus was the prophesied Messiah by pointing out that Jesus did not bring lasting peace to the world. As a matter of fact, they say, His shameful death at the hands of the Romans is the chief evidence of the crushing defeat of any Messianic aspirations He may have entertained. The Jewish leaders have seen the experience of the cross as incompatible with their own Messianic expectations. Paul expressed the problem thus: "We preach Christ crucified, *a stumbling block to Jews* and folly to Gentiles" (1 Cor 1:23).

But what was really the problem: Jesus' failure or a faulty Jewish expectation? Jesus answered that these disciples had not considered *all* that the Hebrew Scriptures had spoken about a *suffering* Messiah. Jesus did not deny that the Scriptures foretold a time of glory when Messiah would bring worldwide peace. He explained that *before* that took place, however, the Messiah must come to suffer. His words were powerful: "Was it not necessary that the Christ (i.e., the Messiah) suffer these things and enter into His glory?" (Luke 24:26). Yes, that was the order: suffering, then glory! The painful events which they had witnessed over the last three days were not evidence that Jesus had failed; they were evidence that He had succeeded in accomplishing the first stage of the redemptive plan! The Scriptures actually had prophesied that He would be rejected and would die a shameful death before His glorification.

It was then that the Master Teacher began a Bible study that must have been a marvel to hear. "And beginning with Moses and all the Prophets, He interpreted to them in all the Scriptures the things concerning Himself" (Luke 24:27). If this writer were able to board a time machine and be transported back to any place in history, it would be back to first century Judea to join this intense study of the Scriptures with the One whom those Scriptures foretold! Although Luke does not tell us the specific passages He discussed, the rest of the New Testament indicates that Jesus likely included such passages as Psalm 22, Isaiah 53 and Zechariah 9:9 in His teaching. No doubt He also expounded upon many more passages as He covered the entire field of Old Testament Messianic prophecy from Moses to Malachi.

Suffering and *glory*! Those two apparently contradictory themes compose the key to unlocking the riches of Old Testament prophecy and the mystery of Messiah's person and work. Peter later wrote that the Hebrew prophets often searched out the relationship between these two seemingly contradictory roles: "inquiring what person or time the Spirit of Messiah in them was indicating when he predicted the sufferings of Messiah and the subsequent glories" (1 Pet 1:11). This much was becoming clear to the disciples: it was God's plan that His Messiah first come as a *lamb* to suffer and die before He would come as a *lion* to conquer and reign.

The effect that this new light had on Cleopas and his companion must have been slow in coming, but later it hit them like the proverbial "ton of bricks." They were fascinated enough with His exegesis to invite Him to join them in a meal. Then, as He was breaking bread with them, "their eyes were opened, and they recognized Him. And He vanished from their sight. They said to each other, 'Did not our hearts burn within us while He talked to us on the road, while He opened the Scriptures to us?'" (Luke 24:31–32).

Nothing less than a "holy heartburn" could describe their reaction to this wonderful approach to the Scriptures which they previously thought they had fully understood. They raced back to relate their experience to the other disciples who were huddling in Jerusalem and suffering from the same discouragement that they had earlier experienced. Then Jesus appeared to the entire group, showed them His wounds and expounded again the Scriptures about His suffering. He showed them what He had shown previously to the two: that His experience of suffering was consistent with the Hebrew Scriptures that all of them revered.

> Then He opened their minds to understand the Scriptures, and said to them, "Thus it is written, that the Messiah should suffer and on the third day rise from the dead, and that repentance and forgiveness of sins should be proclaimed in His name to all nations, beginning from Jerusalem" (Luke 24:45–47).

The lessons arising from these momentous events recorded in Luke 24 are for all people: Jews, Gentiles and the Church of God.

Jewish perplexity and hesitancy regarding Jesus can be cleared up by an honest appraisal of what *all* the Jewish Scriptures foretold about Messiah's coming to suffer and die for sin. Most Jewish people have never taken the time to consider the evidence of fulfilled Messianic prophecy. When they do study the many prophecies that found their fulfillment nearly two thousand years ago, they often conclude with Philip, "We have found Him of whom Moses in the Law and also the prophets wrote, Jesus of Nazareth, the son of Joseph" (John 1:45).

The purpose of the following pages is to explore with the reader the evidence from the Hebrew Scriptures about the person, nature, and mission of the Messiah of Israel. Our special focus will be on the Advent prophecies, but we will also extend our study to later events in the Messiah's life. We will successively examine each prophecy in its context, seeing whether or not the Christian claim that it was fulfilled by Jesus of Nazareth has credibility. We will also try to examine how that Messianic promise developed and was shaped by the events that followed the writing of the Old Testament. That will involve a brief consideration of some events during those roughly four hundred years called the "Intertestamental Period" by Christians. How various Jewish groups responded to Jesus will be discovered. Against the social, cultural and religious background of this period, the Messianic hope will be seen. Finally, we will explore how the unbelieving Jewish community responded to Jesus' message and what attitudes about Him crystallized over the years. It will be an exciting journey through Scripture, history, culture and apologetics. It could also be a life-transforming journey if the reader keeps his mind and heart open to the teaching of the Word of God.

If you have come thus far, I invite you to continue this exploration with me.

My heart rejoices in You, O LORD. I smile at my enemies because I rejoice in Your salvation. No one is holy like You, O LORD, for there is none besides You, nor is there any rock like our God. You, O LORD are a God of knowledge, and by You actions are weighed. You, O LORD kill and make alive. You bring down to the grave and bring up. You make poor and make rich; You bring low and lift up. He raises the poor from the dust and lifts the beggar from the ash heap, to set us among princes and make us inherit the throne of glory. The pillars of the earth are Yours, O LORD, and You have set the world upon them. You will guard the feet of Your saints, but the wicked will be silent in darkness. For by strength no man shall prevail. Your enemies, O LORD will be broken in pieces; from heaven You will thunder against them. You will judge the ends of the earth, and You will give strength to Your king, and exalt the horn of Your Messiah. Amen.

(Adapted from Hannah's prayer in 1 Sam 2:1–10)

CHAPTER 2

A Woman's Seed

Conversations between individuals have often turned the tide of history. A conversation between Roosevelt, Stalin and Churchill decided the fate of millions in post-war Europe. Conversations between a former President and his aides, recorded on tape, led to his resignation and the blot on American history called "Watergate." We all would be surprised if we knew how our everyday lives are affected by the conversations of powerful individuals at the highest levels of national and international caucuses.

The tragic and far-reaching results of a brief encounter in a beautiful garden many years ago have been far beyond those of any other conversation in history. The conversation is recorded for us in Genesis 3, one of the most important of all the many important chapters in the Word of God. And yet, out of the darkness of that episode involving a serpent, a woman, a man, and God shines forth a beacon of hope to a lost world. That beacon, found in the simple but profound words of verse 15, has been called by theologians the "protoevangelium," that is, the first announcement of the good news of the gospel. The words of this promise were addressed by God to the Satanic power behind the serpent:

I will put enmity between you and the woman, and between your offspring and her offspring; He shall crush your head, and you shall crush His heel.

To begin fathoming the depths of meaning embedded in those few words, we must first take a brief look at the preceding events which prompted this momentous promise.

The Conversation with the Woman (Gen 3:1–5)

The man and the woman had been placed in an ideal environment with only one restriction: don't eat from one tree (Gen 2:16–17). That command actually had been given to the man before the woman was created. It was his responsibility to communicate God's words correctly to his wife. This fact must be recognized to fully understand the woman's response to the serpent's question in Genesis 3:1–2.

Employing the instrument of a serpent, Satan launched a two-fold attack on "the woman" (remember that she was not named "Eve" until after the fall; see Gen 3:20). First, Satan attacked the *Word of God*: "Now the serpent was craftier than any other beast of the field which the LORD God had made. He said to the woman, *Did God actually say*, 'You shall not eat of any tree in the garden?'" (Gen 3:1). He sought to cast doubt in her mind about what God had actually said. It was not the truth of God's word that he attacked, but the clarity with which He had spoken to her about His will. Such attacks on the veracity of God's Word have been one of Satan's favorite methods ever since that fateful day in the garden. He is delighted when he can cast doubts about God's Word into the minds of God's creatures. The woman's response sounds good at first, but she added something to the original Divine command: "God said, 'You shall not eat of the fruit of the tree that is in the midst of the garden, *neither shall you touch it*, lest you die'" (Gen 3:3). Evidently, the man had not communicated God's Word faithfully to his wife. Sadly, he must have added the matter about not touching the tree.

Satan's next thrust was to attack the *wisdom of God*: "But the serpent said to the woman, 'You will not surely die. For God knows that when you eat of it your eyes will be opened, and you will be like God, knowing good and evil'" (Gen 3:4–5). Now the enemy launched a frontal attack by directly calling God an outright liar. Furthermore, God's motive was impugned—the serpent alleged that God did not want any creatures to have the kind of knowledge that He alone possessed. The word translated as "God" earlier in the verse is *Elohim* and should be rendered "God" in its second occurrence as well. When this is understood, it is clear that Satan was accusing God of jealousy as well. In other words, God doesn't want anyone to be like Him! Will the woman stand her ground and obey God in light of this twofold attack on the word and wisdom of her Creator?

Committing the Sin (Gen 3:6)

"So when the woman saw that the tree was good for food, and that it was a delight to the eyes, and that the tree was to be desired to make one wise, she took of its fruit and ate, and she also gave some to her husband who was with her, and he ate" (Gen 3:6). The fruit had a threefold appeal to the woman, corresponding to the threefold appeal of the world in 1 John 2:16. The tree was: (1) "good for food" (i.e., "lust of the flesh"); (2) "a delight to the eyes" (i.e., "lust of the eyes"); and (3) "desired to make one wise" (i.e., "pride of life"). The tempter has always approached God's creatures through one of these three human desires.

In a similar way, he utilized the same threefold approach in tempting the second "Adam," the Lord Jesus, recorded in Matthew

4:1–13. There, Satan asked Jesus to turn stones into bread (i.e., "the lust of the flesh"); to cast Himself down from the Temple before a marveling crowd (i.e., "the lust of the eyes"); and to receive the world's kingdoms through worshipping the "prince of this world" (i.e., "the pride of life"). Had the woman responded as Jesus had, by citing the Word of God, she would have been able to thwart the tempter. However, she and her husband succumbed and satisfied their desires. They sacrificed the permanent on the altar of the immediate. And we who are their descendants have fared no better by following their examples.

The Consciousness of the Sin (Gen 3:7–8)

"Then the eyes of both were opened, and they knew that they were naked. And they sewed fig leaves together and made themselves loincloths. And they heard the sound of the LORD God walking in the garden in the cool of the day, and the man and his wife hid themselves from the presence of the LORD God among the trees of the garden."

The results were immediate. Whereas previously each had enjoyed a harmonious personality free from guilt, they now attempted to cover their shame with fig leaves. A Jewish tradition suggests that the unnamed "fruit," so often referred to as an "apple" in popular thought, was most likely a fig since its leaves were used to cover their nakedness. Others have thought it might have been the pomegranate, because of the appearance of that fruit on the High Priest's robe in later days (Exod 28:34). No matter what the specific kind of fruit our parents ate, leaves of a plant were inadequate to remove their guilt. Later in the chapter, the Lord covered the humbled pair with skins, obviously from slain animals. Many have seen in this Divine action a prefiguring of the truth that sinners are restored by blood and not by their own meritorious deeds.

Their consciousness of sin extended not only to themselves but also to God. Whereas previously they had enjoyed close fellowship with the Lord, their new attitude was different. Instead of running to God, they tried to hide from Him. The lesson is simple: sin produces shame. One cannot be practicing sin and at the same time be enjoying that sweet fellowship of unbroken communion with God.

Confronting the Sinners (Gen 3:9–13)

The Lord God then confronted each of the actors in this momentous drama. He first questioned the man concerning his whereabouts and asked if he had eaten of the forbidden tree. God did not ask these questions because He was ignorant. Rather, He wished to elicit a response from Adam. The man, however, responded with the oft-quoted excuse, "The woman whom you gave to be with me, she gave me fruit of the tree, and I ate" (3:12). Thus began the long history of one of the favorite pastimes of fallen humanity, blame-shifting.

The woman, however, was no better in her response. When confronted with the same question, she blamed her actions on the serpent who had "deceived" her (3:13). It is said that President Harry Truman had a sign on his desk proclaiming, "The Buck Stops Here!" Adam and his wife, however, were the founders of the infamous "The Buck Stops *There*" society. And, alas, its members are still among us today! What lasting consequences come when sin is committed!

The Consequences of the Sin (Gen 3:14–24)

The rest of this chapter can be summarized in three parts: (1) The Pronouncements of Judgment (3:14–19); (2) The Provision of Covering (3:20–22); and (3) The Precaution against Eating (3:23–24). What will concern us in this chapter, however, is the series of sentences pronounced on the three guilty parties. The man must toil in physical labor (3:17–19) while the woman must toil in maternal labor (3:16). Before these pronouncements, however, the Lord promises judgment on the serpent:

> The LORD God said to the serpent, "Because you have done this, cursed are you above all livestock and above all beasts of the field; on your belly you shall go, and dust you shall eat all the days of your life. I will put enmity between you and the woman, and between your offspring and her offspring; He shall bruise your head, and you shall bruise His heel" (3:14–15).

Embedded within these ominous words of doom is mankind's only hope: the seed of the woman, the Deliverer, the Savior, the Messiah. The promise declares that the *coming one* will not arrive, however, before a fierce conflict develops. Here is not only a promise of hope but also of warfare; it will be a battle between followers of the Lord and of Satan. Ultimately, the conflict will focus on two individuals. The word "seed" or "offspring" in Hebrew (*zerah*) has both a collective and an individual meaning, just like its English equivalent. The singular pronoun used in the promise, "*He* shall bruise your head," indicates that a male member of the human race will deliver a fatal and final blow to the serpent. Medieval religious art often painted Mary as crushing the serpent underfoot, due to the translation of "he" as "she" in the early Latin translation called the Vulgate. But this is simply a wrong translation of Gen 3:15 because the Hebrew pronoun as well as its Greek translation in the Septuagint is clearly masculine. Eve's male descendant will crush the serpent's head, but this final blow will not come without the woman's offspring also receiving a bruise on His heel.

Until modern times, Jewish commentators saw a prophecy of the coming Messiah in this verse. Consider, for example, this comment from *Bereshit Rabba* 23, a rabbinic commentary on Genesis: "Eve had respect to that seed which is coming from another place. And who is this? This is Messiah the King." In the light of later revelation in the Hebrew Bible and its fulfillment in the New Testament, the general and rather mysterious truths of this promise shine brightly to the eye of faith. Basically, this verse teaches that Messiah will suffer in the process of finally defeating Satan. The concept of a suffering Messiah, although unfamiliar to many Jewish people, can be traced back to this ancient promise. Isaiah further developed this theme with his teaching about the *suffering servant*. Consider Isaiah 53:5: "He was wounded for our transgressions; He was crushed for our iniquities," and Isaiah 53:10a: "Yet it was the will of the LORD to crush Him."

The New Testament is clear that Messiah accomplished this victory at the cross. Consider, for example, Hebrews 2:14–15: "Since therefore the children share in flesh and blood, He Himself likewise partook of the same things, that through death He might destroy the one who has the power of death, that is, the devil, and deliver all those who through fear of death were subject to lifelong slavery." The New Testament is also clear that the final punishment and total disabling of Satan await the end times. "The God of peace will soon crush Satan under your feet" (Rom 16:20). The Book of Revelation portrays this final fulfillment as taking place at the Great White Throne Judgment (Rev 20:11–15). It is clear that while Satan is truly alive, he is not well on planet earth! He is a defeated foe, although his final doom awaits him.

In conclusion, what basic truths can be deduced about the advent of the Messiah from Genesis 3:15? First, Messiah will be of *unique birth*: He will be *the seed of the woman*, not *of the man*. We can then rightly see a prediction of the virgin birth in this promise, although we should be patient with someone who has difficulty seeing this truth. Second, Messiah will be *supernatural*: He will defeat Satan, a supernatural being. Only one who has power beyond that of mere man can defeat him who is called "the prince of the power of the air" (Eph 2:2). Thus, Messiah's *deity* is implied. Third, Messiah will be of the *human race*: from a woman, not an angel or a visitor from another world. Thus, the ultimate mystery begins to unfold: that Messiah will be both God and man, a theme later developed by the prophets (Isa 9:6; Jer 23:5–6; Mic 5:2).

It must be kept in mind that this promise is only the beginning of a long series of Messianic prophecies. As revelation unfolds, more information will come forth and Messiah's credentials will progressively narrow the focus on one who will also be a descendant of Shem (Gen 9:26), of Abraham (Gen 12:3), of Isaac (Gen 26:3), of Jacob (Gen 35:11–12), of Judah (Gen 49:10), of David (2 Sam 7:12–16), of Zerubbabel (Hag 2:23), and who will be born in Bethlehem (Mic 5:2) before the Temple is destroyed (Dan 9:24–26; AD 70). Like an inverted pyramid, this portrait of Messiah rests on the only One who could fit these and the many other prophecies concerning Him: Jesus of Nazareth, born of a woman (Gal 4:4), who vanquished Satan and who sets free those who are in Satanic bondage (Heb 2:14–15).

As sweet and beautiful are the pastoral scenes in that Nativity in Bethlehem, the larger message is that on this evening the battle has been launched on planet earth! The advent initiated a spiritual war that will not be finished until Satan himself is destroyed (Revelation 20). But we are getting ahead of ourselves. There is much more to examine about this powerful promised deliverer before that final act unfolds!

May the LORD answer us in the day of our trouble and may the name of the God of Jacob defend us. May He send us help from the sanctuary and strengthen us out of Zion; May He grant us our heart's desire and fulfill all His purposes. We will rejoice in your salvation, and in the name of our God we will set up our banners! May the LORD fulfill all our petitions. Now I know that the LORD saves His Messiah and will answer Him from His holy heaven with the saving strength of His right hand. Some trust in chariots, and some in horses, but we will remember your name, O LORD our God. Many have bowed down and fallen, but we have risen and stand upright. Save us, LORD! May the King answer us when we call. Amen.

(Adapted from Psalm 20)

CHAPTER 3

A Lion or a Lamb

If a poll were taken to determine which of Jacob's twelve sons were the most famous, certainly either Joseph or Judah would be the favored one. Although more space is given in the Scriptures to the personal history of Joseph than any of his brothers (Gen 37–50), far more is said about the tribe of Judah than any other tribe. Genesis 49 records the death bed "blessings" of the dying Jacob, spoken over his twelve boys. The atmosphere was electric as each son awaited his special inheritance. What will Dad bequeath to me?

Reuben, through his unstable act of immorality, had forfeited his position as firstborn among his brothers (Gen 49:3–4). That Joseph and Judah were the benefactors of this forfeiture is clearly stated in 1 Chronicles 5:1–2: "The sons of Reuben the firstborn of Israel (for he was the firstborn, but because he defiled his father's couch, his birthright was given to the sons of Joseph the son of Israel, so that he could not be enrolled as the oldest son; though Judah became strong among his brothers and a chief came from him, yet the birthright belonged to Joseph)." Reuben's right to the double inheritance was forfeited to Joseph, and his right to the position of leadership over his brothers was forfeited to Judah.

The two longest patriarchal blessings in Genesis 49 are reserved for Judah and Joseph. Judah's blessing is recorded in Genesis 49:8-12.

It follows the prophecies on his three older brothers, Reuben, Simeon and Levi, each of whom had committed questionable moral acts affecting Jacob's commentaries regarding them (see Gen 35:22 and 34:25–31). In contrast to those prophecies of doom on Reuben, Simeon and Levi are the series of prophetic blessings pronounced upon Judah and his descendants.

> Judah, your brothers shall praise you. Your hand shall be on the neck of your enemies; your father's sons shall bow down to you. Judah is a lion's whelp; from the prey, my son, you have gone up. He couches, he lies down as a lion, and as a lion, who dares rouse him up? The scepter shall not depart from Judah, nor the ruler's staff from between his feet, until Shiloh comes, and to him *shall be* the obedience of the peoples (Gen 49:8–10).

Four prophecies about Judah appear in these verses.

Judah Will Be the Leader of His Brothers

In this amazing series of blessings, Jacob often employed a play on words. Judah means "praise" (see Gen 29:35). Thus, he will be praised by his brothers who will recognize his leadership. Judah appears to have assumed this leadership role during his lifetime. In Genesis 37:26–27, we are told he helped to spare Joseph's life by suggesting that the brothers sell him to the Ishmaelites rather than kill him. When the brothers later went down into Egypt and were unknowingly cared for by their brother Joseph, Judah was the spokesman for the group (Gen 44:14–34).

In subsequent years, as the tribes were marching through the wilderness, it was the tribe of Judah that went first (Num 10:14). After the Israelites conquered the land of Canaan and began to possess it, "the allotment for the tribe of the people of Judah" was received first (Josh 15:1). The tribe of Judah was allotted the largest and most important sections of the Promised Land in the southern part of the land of Canaan. Numbers chapters 1 and 26 list two censuses taken of the tribes of Israel, one at the beginning and one at the end of the forty-year wanderings. In both censuses, Judah had the largest population of any of the tribes.

Judah, therefore, was the leading brother and later the leading tribe. Toward the end of the Old Testament period, the tribe of Judah lent its name to be one of the names for all the Israelite people – the "Judeans" or simply, the "Jews."

Judah Will Be a Great Conqueror

Jacob said to Judah: "your hand shall be on the neck of your enemies" (Gen 49:8b). This is a graphic reference to the humiliation of one's enemies in battle. To expose the neck of one's enemy was a symbolic act signifying that the enemy had been conquered (Josh 10:24).

The greatest conqueror in the history of Israel was King David, a descendant of Judah. David himself composed a beautiful song, in which he praised God for giving him strength, particularly in battle. It is interesting that he used the very phrase employed by Jacob in this prophecy: "You have also given me the necks of my enemies, so that I destroyed those who hated me" (2 Sam 22:41; Ps 18:40, NKJV).

In this regard, Judah is compared to a lion. "Judah is a lion's whelp; from the prey, my son, you have gone up. He couches, he lies down as a lion. And as a lion, who dares rouse him up?" (Gen 49:9). The kingly character of Judah mentioned in verse 10 is appropriately symbolized by the lion who is often called the king of beasts. This theme is carried through the Scriptures, even into the New Testament. Revelation 5:5 describes a scene in the throne room of Heaven in which the lion of the tribe of Judah is the main character. This is a Messianic reference to the Lord Jesus Christ who, by descent, was a member of this tribe. The passage in Revelation, however, introduces another animal into this mix. When John turns to see that lion, he then sees a lamb as slain (5:6). The seeming contradiction between the nature of those two animals actually portrays a Messianic irony: the one whose Messianic credentials described Him as a lion was in His actual redeeming work a sacrificial lamb! You see, it is not really a question of whether He will be a lion or a lamb. The truth is that He will be both!

Judah Will Produce a Royal Line of Kings

"The scepter shall not depart from Judah, nor a lawgiver from between his feet, until Shiloh come; and unto him shall be the obedience of the peoples" (Gen 49:10). Although the early government of Israel was a theocracy rather than a monarchy, the Lord anticipated that there one day would be kings in Israel (Deut 17:14–20). In later years, the first king of Israel, Saul, was from the tribe of Benjamin, but he was replaced by David (1 Sam 16:1–13). All the legitimate kings of Judah throughout her history were descendants of David. Jacob's prophecy stated that the symbols of royalty, the scepter and the ruler's staff, would never depart from Judah. This teaches that the right to reign as king will always be with the tribe of Judah.

Verse 10 further states that the scepter will not depart "until Shiloh come." Many have interpreted this phrase to mean that when Shiloh comes, the scepter will depart. This, however, is not what the verse is teaching. No mention is made of a time when the scepter will depart from Judah. The word "until" in the phrase "until Shiloh comes" does not imply termination. The same word is used in God's promise to Jacob recorded in Genesis 28:15: "Behold, I am with you and will keep you wherever you go and will bring you back to this land. For I will not leave you until I have done what I have promised you." God's assurance that He would not leave Jacob until He fulfilled the promise does not mean that He left him when the promise was fulfilled. In reality, the scepter has never departed from Judah. The promise given in Genesis 49:10 is not that the scepter will leave Judah but that in Judah it will reach its greatest glory and extent.

This brings us to a consideration of the last promise given to Judah.

Judah Will Produce the Messiah

Genesis 49:10 promises that one day "Shiloh" will come, as a result of which there is an additional prophecy: "And to him *shall be* the obedience of the peoples." Who, or what, is meant by the term "Shiloh"? Of the many attempts which have been made to interpret the meaning of this word, let us consider the three main approaches to the meaning and referent of "Shiloh" that are mentioned in most of the commentaries.

1. Some believe it refers to the town in Israel named "Shiloh." The most recent Jewish translation of the Scriptures entitled *The Tanakh* states that a literal translation of this verse is "until he comes to Shiloh." The town of Shiloh was the place where the Israelites set up the Tabernacle after the conquest (Josh 18:1). It was the center of Israelite worship until the days of Samuel (1 Sam 1:3). However, to render "Shiloh" in Genesis 49:10 as referring to this town simply results in confusion, since no king ever came "to Shiloh." This interpretation is simply a reflection of the desire to prevent this verse from referring to the Messiah and has no basis in the text itself.

2. The second school of thought interprets the meaning of "Shiloh" as *to whom it belongs* and represents a reference to the Messiah to whom the scepter belongs. Often, the parallel passage of Ezekiel 21:27 is cited as support of this view: "A ruin! A ruin! I will make it a ruin! It will not be restored until he comes *to whom it rightfully belongs*; to him I will give it" (NIV). The ancient Greek translation, called the Septuagint, interpreted "Shiloh" in this way. However, to translate "Shiloh" as *to whom it belongs* requires changing one of the consonants of the Hebrew word. When interpreters begin to alter the text of Scripture to favor their interpretation, they are on dangerous ground. Although this interpretation does see the verse as referring to the Messiah, it is questionable to say the least.

3. The best interpretation views "Shiloh" as a personal name of the Messiah (i.e., the right of kingship will always be with Judah until the Messiah comes). To Him (that is, the Messiah) the nations will submit. The Talmud lists "Shiloh" as one of the names of Messiah (*Sanhedrin* 98b). The most ancient Jewish commentary on the Book of Genesis also adopts this interpretation (*Bereshit Rabba* 99). This is the view of a number of English translations (NASB, KJV, NKJV) and of many evangelical commentators. The name "Shiloh" easily could be related to the word *shalom*, the Hebrew word for *peace*. This would be consistent with the prophecy of the Messiah's coming in Isaiah 9:6 and Micah 5:5:

> "For to us a child is born, to us a son is given; and the government shall be upon His shoulder, and His name shall be called Wonderful Counselor, Mighty God, Everlasting Father, *Prince of Peace*" (Isa 9:6).

> "And He shall be their *peace*" (Mic 5:5).

This interpretation is preferred above the others since it represents the simple rendering of the Hebrew text as it stands.

Undoubtedly, the word "Shiloh" refers to the King Messiah— an interpretation affirmed even by the great medieval Jewish commentator, Rashi. This prophecy is one more stroke in the developing portrait of the Messiah in the Old Testament Scriptures. From that time on, people looked for the Promised One to come from the tribe of Judah. Let us rehearse again the family tree of the Messiah which we have noted in previous chapters. In Genesis 3:15, we are told simply that the deliverer will come from mankind (the seed of the woman). In Genesis 9:26, another characteristic is mentioned: He will be a descendant of Shem, one of the three sons of Noah. Years later, God again narrowed His genealogy by saying that among the descendants of Shem, Abraham would be the ancestor of Him in whom all families of the earth would be blessed (Gen 12:3). That Messianic line was further narrowed to one of the two sons of Abraham, namely Isaac (Gen 21:12). The Messianic line was again narrowed to one of the two sons of Isaac, namely Jacob (Gen 25:23). Of Jacob's twelve sons, Judah was chosen as the one through whom the Messiah would come (2 Sam 7:12–16). Then the genealogy was narrowed once more when a specific town within Judah, Bethlehem, was chosen as the site of Messiah's birth (Mic 5:2).

This is but a brief outline of the Messianic credentials. Anyone claiming to be the Messiah must present these credentials to Israel. Jesus possessed these credentials. In Matthew 1:1–16, the genealogy of Jesus is listed and clearly shows Him as one who genealogically qualifies to be the Messiah. The marvelous account in Matthew 2:1–10 of the birth of Jesus in Bethlehem was in accordance with Micah 5:2. Jesus presented to Israel as their Messiah these and many more credentials.

But someone may ask, *Could a Jewish person appear in the future who would have these same credentials and be Israel's Messiah?* No, he could not, because there are no records available to substantiate such a claim. When the Romans destroyed Jerusalem in AD 70, the Temple, with all of its treasures and archives, was completely destroyed as well. One of the treasures of the Temple was the records necessary to validate the family and tribal genealogies. Since that fateful day, no Jewish person has been able to prove by written records his or her ancient genealogy.

When this author was doing graduate work at a Jewish college in Philadelphia, I was privileged to study under an Orthodox Jewish professor with a PhD from Harvard University. She taught me medieval Jewish history for 30 consecutive weeks through the school year. The most interesting fact about that experience was that I was the only student in the class! Therefore, we had plenty of opportunities to explore issues in depth, without the pressure of other class members.

Each week I was required to read 400 to 500 pages on a given topic. My professor and I would then discuss the issue in class. About halfway through the year, the subject for the week was "The Messiah in Medieval Judaism." When I arrived for class, my professor, knowing my evangelical convictions, said, "Well, Mr. Varner (I was not a Doctor then), I guess you've been waiting for this week for quite a while. Mr. Varner, let me explain one thing. In my opinion, Christianity is totally irrational and highly mystical, and I cannot see how any thinking person can believe it."

Since she threw down the gauntlet, I decided to pick it up and accept the challenge. I answered, "Do you mind if I take a few minutes and share with you the reasons why I believe the Christian faith has solid reasons for its validity?" She said, "Sure, go right ahead." So for the next half hour she allowed me to make my case for the Messiahship of Jesus and the truth of the New Testament. I mentioned each Messianic prophecy and fulfillment I could bring to mind. I brought out arguments for the resurrection and the validity of the New Testament. God gave me great boldness.

I finished by telling her, "If Jesus is not the Messiah, then Orthodox Jews will be very disappointed because *there will be no future Messiah for Israel.*" Shocked at this, she asked what I meant by such a remark. I reminded her of what she already knew, that the genealogical records had been destroyed, and no one claiming to be the Messiah today can authenticate it by producing the genealogical records. Then my learned professor answered, "Certainly somebody somewhere has kept the records." Even though she had no idea who or where that "somebody" was who supposedly has the records, she expressed the hope that they someday could be produced to authenticate the claims of her future Messiah. Again she remarked, "I certainly hope somebody has kept the records because I sure want to know Him when He comes."

I then concluded, "But you know that nobody has kept the records. Jesus claimed to be the Messiah before the records were destroyed. No one at that time questioned His genealogical descent from Judah and David. The only credentials He will bring with Him at His second coming will be the wounds which He received at His first coming" (cf. Zech 12:10).

If Jesus is not the fulfillment of the "Shiloh" passage in Genesis 49:10, the sober fact facing Israel is that there never will be anyone who can prove that he fulfills the prophecies of Messiah's royal lineage. But there is one who meets all these qualifications—the Lion of Judah who is also the Lamb slain to redeem Jews and Gentiles from sin's bondage. See both the amazing contrast of a lion and a lamb and also their identical continuity so powerfully expressed in Rev 5:5–10.

As odd as it may sound, on that first Christmas night a lion roared and a lamb bleated!

———————▼———————

My soul magnifies the Lord, and my spirit has rejoiced in God my Savior. For He has regarded the lowly state of His handmaid; for behold, henceforth all generations will call us blessed. For He who is mighty has done great things for us, and holy is His name. His mercy is on those who fear Him from generation to generation. He has shown strength with His arm and He has scattered the proud in the imagination of their hearts. He has put down the mighty from their thrones and exalted the lowly. He has filled the hungry with good things, and the rich He has sent away empty. He has helped His servant Israel in remembrance of His mercy, as He spoke to our fathers, to Abraham and to his seed forever. Amen.

(Adapted from Mary's prayer in Luke 1:46–55)

CHAPTER 4

A Star and a Scepter

A nyone who has traveled with small children will remember the question that inevitably arises from at least one of them during a trip, "Are we almost there?" Sometimes the query is, "How much longer before we get there?" These and similar inquiries often are voiced by eager young ones only fifteen minutes into an extended trip!

Can you imagine how many times these questions were heard from little children during the Israelites' forty-year journey to the Promised Land? Not only the children who came out of Egypt, but also *their* children must have asked those questions hundreds of times. The answer they most often probably received was, "We don't know **when** but we do know **that** God will lead us to our land someday."

When the Israelites finally reached the plains of Moab, however, that answer must have changed to "**Soon** we will be there, children." The plains of Moab were "beyond the Jordan at Jericho" (Num 22:1). The people could look across the narrow river in its gorge and see the Promised Land. It had been a long and tedious journey, and they now were almost home. They had endured dozens of trials and conflicts during their wilderness experience, but as they were camped on those plains, they would experience the most severe attack of all. The ironic thing about this trial, however, is that none of the Israelites—not even Moses—knew anything about it when it was taking place!

Numbers 22–24 records the account of Balaam, the seer from the east, who was hired to curse Israel but ended up only blessing them. This fascinating, yet perplexing, account was considered so important by ancient Jews that the rabbis in the Talmud referred to this section as the sixth book of Moses! A current evangelical scholar also has written, "Many Old Testament theologians have seen in the Balaam narrative the quintessence of the theology of the Pentateuch" (Ronald Allen, in *Tradition and Testament,* [Moody, 1981], 83).

Who was this Balaam? What did he say about Israel? What did he also say, if anything, about Israel's Deliverer? And is it really possible that this Gentile could foretell the Jewish Messiah? To put it simply, Balaam was a pagan soothsayer from the ancient region known as Mesopotamia (Num 22:5; cf. also Deut 23:4 and Josh 13:22). When Balak, king of Moab, saw the Israelites passing through his land, he knew he could not defeat them militarily. One of the ironies of this account is that Balak's fear of Israel was actually groundless because God already had told Moses not to harm the Moabites (Deut 2:9). Nevertheless, Balak sent a group of messengers to "hire" Balaam to come and curse the Israelites so they could then be beaten.

Balaam must be seen as one of those non-Israelite individuals who had preserved some knowledge of the true God. Other examples in the Pentateuch are Melchizedek (Gen 14:18–20) and Jethro, Moses' father-in-law (Exod 18:1). Many also believe that Job was not of Israelite ancestry. In Balaam's case, however, his information about the true God was mingled with pagan concepts of polytheism.

The account in Numbers 22:8–22 about God's forbidding Balaam to go, then allowing him to go, and then being angry with him for going has perplexed many readers. Although Balaam's initial response seems to be noble ("Go to your own land, for the

LORD has refused to let me go with you," Num 22:13), it must be understood that Balaam longed deeply for the monetary reward and was motivated by covetousness and greed. Both Jewish tradition and the New Testament join in exposing the sinful heart of this man. Consider, for example, this statement in the Talmud: "Those who have an evil eye, an arrogant spirit, and a greedy soul are among the disciples of the wicked Balaam. His disciples inherit Gehenna [i.e., Hell] and descend into the well of destruction" (*Abot* 5:22). The three New Testament references to him are all bad: 2 Peter 2:15 warns of the greedy "way of Balaam"; Jude 11 describes the covetous "error of Balaam"; while Revelation 2:14 exposes the evil "teaching of Balaam."

In light of this, we should view God's anger at Balaam in the account in light of God's knowledge of Balaam's true heart condition. The nineteenth century commentator George Bush (NOT one of the Presidents!) has aptly remarked, "Balaam's heart was set on going; and as the divine wisdom allows men always to act in freedom, so here it is permitted Balaam to go, seeing he was so fully bent upon it" (*Notes on Numbers* [James & Klock, 1976], 350). Perhaps a parallel reference would be Psalm 81:12: "So I gave them over to their stubborn hearts, to follow their own counsels."

On his way, however, the "angel of the LORD" three times impeded Balaam's progress, although Balaam himself could not see him at all (Num 22:22–35). Balaam's donkey, however, was able to see the angel all the while. When Balaam had struck his recalcitrant animal for the third time, "the LORD opened the mouth of the donkey, and she said to Balaam, 'What have I done to you, that you have struck me these three times?'" (22:28). This famous incident is usually all that most Christians know about the Balaam story. While affirming the absolutely historical character of this miracle, it should be noted that most readers often miss another example of irony in this account. The lowly donkey is able to *see* the angel, while the so-called "seer" is blind to the presence of a real spiritual being! This rebuke, from a normally dumb beast at that, must have further humbled Balaam's proud heart. In other words, God's message to him through this incident was, "Your **seeing** is not going to accomplish anything. I will put the words into your mouth."

When Balaam finally arrived, he knew that he could only speak a message from God. He would not be allowed to follow his covetous heart and fulfill Balak's wishes. Yet Balak, probably in desperation, still made elaborate sacrificial preparations for Balaam to proceed with the ritual of cursing (Num 22:39–23:2).

The Prophecies of Balaam (Numbers 23–24)

These two chapters record four separate prophecies uttered by Balaam. It is extremely vital at this point to recognize that it was the Lord, and not Balaam himself, who was the source of these sublime utterances. Before each of the "oracles," it is clearly stated that the Lord put these words into Balaam's mouth (Num 23:5, 16; 24:2, 15–16). Balaam was simply a channel for God's word to be communicated. It is obvious that his heart did not coincide with his words in this regard. Just as God employed a donkey's mouth to deliver a message to Balaam, so He used Balaam's mouth to deliver these marvelous words about the people of Israel.

Most scholars recognize at least four "oracles" in these chapters, each of which is preceded by the words "And Balaam took up his discourse and said" (Num 23:7, 18; 24:3, 15). Each of the messages has to do with some aspect of Israel's position and calling before God and the nations. Each of the "oracles" also thoroughly frustrated Balak, who was hearing just the opposite of what he had hired Balaam to utter—another ironic element in the account. What frustrated Balak so much? There are four themes portrayed in these prophecies.

The Peculiarity of Israel (Num 23:7–10)

Balaam stated that it is impossible to curse what God has blessed (23:8). The reason he was unsuccessful in cursing Israel was that this people was unique, unlike other *goyim* (i.e., *nations*). "For from the top of the crags I see him, from the hills I behold him; behold, a people dwelling alone, and not counting itself among the nations!" (23:9). This special calling of Israel is the explanation for Israel's *persecution* by others down through the years. Those who hate Israel do so because they are "different" in their own eyes. Deuteronomy 7:6 declares about this people: "For you are a people holy to the LORD your God. The LORD your God has chosen you to be a people for His treasured possession, out of all the peoples who are on the face of the earth." Anti-Semites refuse to acknowledge this uniqueness and end up fighting against God's purpose in history and redemption.

This special peculiarity of Israel is also the explanation for its *preservation* during its long and dark night of exile in strange lands. Try as they may, those who attempt to annihilate Israel cannot destroy it. Israel's continued existence, despite unbelievable suffering, will endure as long as the sun, moon and stars are ordinances in the heavens (Jer 31:35–36). If someone is able to destroy those ordinances, then they will be able to destroy this special people. It is obvious, therefore, that Israel cannot be destroyed.

The Position of Israel (Num 23:18–24)

Balaam declared that God was not going to change His mind (23:19). He views Israel in a special way. "He has not beheld misfortune in Jacob, nor has He seen trouble in Israel. The LORD their God is with them, and the shout of a king is among them" (23:21). Israel's blessing is based on her unique relationship to the Lord. He is "with" them and, because of that position, He does not see their "trouble" or "wickedness." Even though Israel's *practice* often fell far short of obedience, Israel's *position* was secure. This is Israel's *standing* before the Lord, even though Israel's actual *state* may at times be quite different.

There is a parallel to the New Testament believer's *position* in Christ, but there is also a difference. The Old Testament picture is that the Lord was *with* Israel, while the New Testament picture is that the believer is *in* the Lord. In both cases, however, positional truth allows God to view both Old Testament believers and New Testament believers as beautiful in His sight.

The Privilege of Israel (Num 24:3-9)

It is in this sublime utterance that the absolute principle of the Abrahamic Covenant is reiterated. "Blessed are those who bless you, and cursed are those who curse you" (24:9b). Balaam is simply reminding Balak of what God had already stated to Abraham (Gen 12:3) and reiterated to Isaac (Gen 27:29). The significance of the Abrahamic Covenant in Old Testament theology cannot be overstated. The Balaam account is a frontal attack on the foundational blessing for Israel, originally given to Abram, their father: "I will bless you" (see Gen 12:1–3). Balak and all other "Israel-cursers," however, are here reminded that they actually call God's curse on their own heads when they curse God's people, Israel.

It seems that throughout history whenever a mighty prince attempted to curse Israel, the Jews ended up with another holiday! Pharaoh attempted to smite Israel's children, and the Jews were eventually given the holiday of Passover (Exod 1–12). Haman schemed to destroy all the Jews in the Persian Empire, and the Jews were eventually given the holiday of Purim (recorded in the Book of Esther). The Syrian tyrant Antiochus attempted to murder and assimilate his Jewish subjects, and the Jews were eventually given the festival of Hanukkah (recorded in the Apocryphal book of 1 Maccabees). Even the evil Hitler, although excising a portion of the Jewish body, eventually committed suicide. Only three years later the Jews celebrated their own Independence Day, when the modern state of Israel was born, rising like a Phoenix from its ashes! This principle can also be seen in the hateful effort of Herod to destroy the newborn Messiah (Matt 2:1–12). He destroyed others by death, but in the end he died a miserable death. The kingdom of the hateful Herod eventually disappeared. The kingdom of the target of his hatred is forever and ever!

When will the rest of the Balaks, Persians, Greeks, Romans, Czars, and Nazis learn this simple lesson: "Blessed are those who bless you, and cursed are those who curse you" (24:9b)?

The Prince of Israel (Num 24:14–24)

Balak had reached his limit. He had hired Balaam to curse Israel, but all he ever did was bless them! In total frustration he ordered Balaam to return home—without his wages (Num 24:10–11)! God, however, was not through. He placed one more message in Balaam's mouth: the most sublime of his four utterances. This "oracle" focused on the ultimate fulfillment of blessing on Israel through a personal Deliverer from all her enemies. "I see him, but not now; I behold him, but not near: a star shall come out of Jacob, and a scepter shall rise out of Israel; it shall crush the forehead of Moab and break down all the sons of Sheth" (Num 24:17). The Hebrew parallelism of this verse makes it clear that Balaam saw one individual in the distant future who would arise out of the Jewish people and destroy the descendants of the very nation represented by Balak (i.e., the Moabites).

Two graphic pictures are employed to describe this individual: a
star and a scepter. Both of these figures of speech point to an illus-
trious and powerful king. The Jewish sect at Qumran, which produced the Dead Sea Scrolls, made much of this description of King-
Messiah as a *star*. Furthermore, the Jewish military leader Simon
ben Kosiba was mistakenly hailed as Messiah in AD 132 and called
"Bar Cochba," literally *son of the star*. More importantly, Jesus takes
this title in Revelation 22:16: "I, Jesus, have sent my angel to testify
to you about these things for the churches. I am the root and the
descendant of David, the bright morning star." When the Magi
came from Mesopotamia (the same area as their ancestor Balaam),
they desired to find the King of the Jews, "For we saw his star when
it rose and have come to worship him." (Matt 2:2b). It was Balaam's
prophecy of a star to which they undoubtedly were referring.

The mention of a scepter also calls to mind a Messianic king.
This verse is practically an echo of what we earlier saw in that
promise to Judah: "The *scepter* shall not depart from Judah, nor a
lawgiver from between his feet, until Shiloh come; and unto him
shall the gathering of the people be" (Gen 49:10). In still another
Messianic prophecy, a scepter appears in the hand of the Messiah: "The LORD sends forth from Zion your strong scepter. Rule
in the midst of your enemies!" (Ps 110:2).

While some interpreters have tried to assign the fulfillment of
this prophecy to King David (see 2 Sam 8:2), the language of the
passage goes beyond the limited conquests of David's day. These
marvelous conquests will have their final fulfillment only in the
glorious advent of Messiah at which time He will personally destroy Israel's enemies (Obad 17–21; Zech 14:3, 12; Rev 19:17–21).
Thus, Balaam's prophecies close with a final graphic irony. While
Moab hired Balaam to destroy Israel, Balaam declared that Israel
will actually destroy Moab!

Not only did later interpreters apply this prophecy to King
Messiah, but it is fascinating that an OT writing prophet evidently

looked back to Num 24 as Messianic. It was the prophet Amos in chapters 9:11–12 of his book: "'In that day I will raise up the fallen booth of David, and wall up its breaches; I will also raise up its ruins and rebuild it as in the days of old; that they may possess the remnant of Edom and all the nations who are called by My name,' declares the LORD who does this" (NASB). The Messianic vision of Amos is the same as that of the unlikely "prophet" Balaam. The promised Davidic king (Jesus) will victoriously rule over Israel's enemies when He establishes the outward rule of His Messianic kingdom.

The utterly fascinating account of Balaam thus provides another link in the chain of the Messianic hope of Israel! Not only will the Messiah be the seed of the woman (Gen 3:15), He will be from the tribe of Judah (Gen 49:10) and also a conquering King (Num 24:17). Jesus urged His hearers to find Him in the Hebrew Bible: "You search the Scriptures because you think that in them you have eternal life; and it is they that bear witness about Me" (John 5:39). And we are seeing Him emerge in these early Pentateuchal oracles!

———————▼———————

 Blessed be the Lord God of Israel, for He has visited and redeemed His people, and has raised up a horn of salvation for us in the house of His servant David. Your holy prophets have spoken that we should be saved from our enemies and from the hand of all who hate us, to perform the mercy promised to our fathers and to remember His holy covenant, the oath which He swore to our father Abraham: to serve Him without fear, in holiness and righteousness before Him all the days of our lives. John went before the face of the Lord to prepare the way of the Messiah, who gave us salvation by the remission of our sins, through Your tender mercy, through Whom the Dayspring from on high has visited us, to give light to those who sit in darkness and the shadow of death, and to guide our feet into the way of peace. Amen.

(Adapted from Zechariah's prayer in Luke 1:68–79)

CHAPTER 5

A House of Bread

When I was a pastor in Pennsylvania (many moons ago!), I was invited to speak to a local Kiwanis meeting in Willow Grove, PA. I chose to speak on why America should be supportive of Israel. Unbeknown to me, there was a Jewish businessman present who was moved by my talk. He mentioned me to his rabbi and soon I received a phone call from that rabbi inviting me to speak at a dinner in his synagogue on a "Brotherhood Day" where non-Jews were invited. I prepared fervently and spoke to the mixed group on the subject "What Jews Should Know about Christians and What Christians Should Know about Jews." I then sneaked in the gospel sideways by explaining what we all need to know about reality! I sat by that rabbi at the meal, and he even offered me a bobby pin to keep the yarmulke from sliding off my bald head. It didn't help!

After the dinner, I had a wonderful conversation with the rabbi in which I was able to share the gospel through the Messianic prophecies. As I mentioned these texts, he said that he wished he had studied the Bible in that way, referring to how I was citing individual texts and quoting them. In the interchange he asked for one prophecy that showed that Jesus was the Messiah of Israel. Micah 5:2 came to my mind, and I quoted, "But as for you, Bethlehem Ephrathah, *too* little to be among the clans of

Judah, From you One will go forth for Me to be ruler in Israel. His goings forth are from long ago, from the days of eternity." So I said that Jesus was born in Bethlehem as a descendant of Judah and was the prophesied King Messiah. Immediately the rabbi shot back, "Oh that is not referring to Jesus—it is a reference to King David who was also born in Bethlehem."

At this point, I ask, how would you respond to that rabbi if he said this to you? But instead of telling you what I said, let's postpone that to the end of this chapter and first look more closely at the meaning of Micah 5:2, a verse that was also mentioned to the Magi when they asked where the Messiah would be born (Matt 2:4–6). I promise you that we will return to that question, but first let's look at that verse in more detail and address the question, "Can it really refer to Jesus or have we just dreamed that up when it really refers to David?

First what is the background of Micah? This is important because, as the saying goes, a text taken out of context can become a pretext for "proving" all sorts of wrong ideas! It is everywhere agreed that the lesser-known prophet Micah was a contemporary of the more well-known prophet Isaiah. Both of them ministered in the eighth century BC. Now remember that universally acknowledged fact, because you will need that information later! Reminiscent of the old story of the city mouse and the country mouse, Isaiah was the city prophet (in the well-known city of Jerusalem) while Micah was the country prophet (in the rarely mentioned village of Moreshet Gath). In addition to being contemporaries, they also share a common passage, almost word for word (Isa 2:2–4 and Mic 4:1–3, a promise of future worldwide blessings). They both prophesied in the coming shadow of the Assyrian invasion (721 BC). Finally, Micah's passage that we are considering about the birth of Messiah is a parallel to Isaiah's famous passage about a virgin conceiving a child called Immanuel (Isa 7:14).

Having seen the historical background on Micah and Isaiah, next we should look at the immediate context of Micah's promise. It is often overlooked that Bethlehem is almost personified by being directly addressed in 5:2: "But as for you, Bethlehem...from you one will come forth..." In the same way a site is addressed a few verses earlier in chapter four. "As for you, tower of the flock, Hill of the daughter of Zion, to you it will come, even the former dominion will come, the kingdom of the daughter of Jerusalem" (Mic 4:8). The phrase "tower of the flock" is actually a name (*Migdal Eder*) that is mentioned in Genesis 35:21 as the place where the dying Rachel was buried. The church father, Jerome, who lived in Bethlehem, wrote that *Migdal Eder* was 1,000 paces from Bethlehem. The Babylonian Talmud (*Shekalim* 7.4) states that *Migdal Eder* was where lambs were raised for the Passover sacrifices in Jerusalem just a few miles to the north. Just outside Bethlehem was where those nighttime shepherds were described as watching their flocks of sheep in Luke 2:8–20. When one pauses to think about that, the conclusion is very probable that the lambs born near Bethlehem were birthed to be sacrificed in Jerusalem, and another "Lamb" was born there who would also be sacrificed in Jerusalem! As we consider Jewish sources, the Aramaic translation of Micah states that "this is the place where, in the last days, Messiah will be revealed" (Targum Jonathan). Micah 4:8 states that the "former dominion" will be restored as the descendant of David arrives there. That word dominion (*memshalah*) is parallel to the "ruler" (*mashal*) who will come out of Bethlehem in 5:2! The prophecy about *Migdal Eder* finishes with the exile in 5:1 and then picks up again in the more famous text (5:2) where kingship is again related to Bethlehem. Yes, the shepherd David came out of Bethlehem (1 Sam 16:11–12) but 5:2 says that this ruler will be similar and yet different from David.

Let's look again at that promise. "But as for you, Bethlehem Ephrathah, too little to be among the clans of Judah, from you

One will go forth for Me to be ruler in Israel. His goings forth are from long ago, from the days of eternity." This familiar verse offers a positive parenthesis between the suffering and exile mentioned in 5:1 and 5:3. Look at some of its amazing details. Bethlehem is qualified by the term Ephratah which means "fruitful." Certainly an apt title for the fruitful and bountiful fields around Bethlehem. Think of that famous pastoral scene of harvesting and gleaning outside Bethlehem featuring Boaz and Ruth (Ruth 2). Ephratah also seems to be the ancient name for the little town (Gen 35:19 and Ruth 1:2). But it is often overlooked that that second name is probably inserted so readers will not confuse this Bethlehem (Ephratah) with another Bethlehem in Galilee (Josh 19:15). I like to say that when the Lord provided the address for the town where Messiah would be born, He also provided the zip code!

But we have not yet mentioned the meaning of Bethlehem, which means "House of Bread"—hence the title for this chapter. This fruitful area called the House of Bread is the origin of the Bread of Life! Another possible connection back to that site is the contrast with the sadness there. Rachel died giving birth to the boy his father called "Benjamin" (Right Hand Son); Rachel wanted him to be named "Benoni" (Son of my sorrow). Matthew 2 tells us that sorrow would also take place again in Bethlehem with the grieving mothers sorrowing for their children (Matt 2:17–18; Jer 31:15). Yet the One who would come forth from there will turn sorrow into rejoicing!

But Micah 5:2 has more to tell us. Bethlehem is described as "little among the thousands of Judah," although that word "thousands" might be translated better as "clans." It was so small that it was not even listed among the dozens of towns of Judah in Joshua 15. And yet this "little town of Bethlehem" had a significant history even before the Messiah was born there. And that history was often marked by pain and tragedy. We have already mentioned that Rachel died in childbirth near this town and Jeremiah mentioned Rachel's female "descendants" were weeping for their own exiled children there (Jer 31:15). Furthermore, what could be called "the R-rated" section of Judges 17–21 twice mentions a man leaving Bethlehem and tragedy follows him. Immediately following is the Book of Ruth which has a lovely ending but which records some truly painful events in chapter one! It appears that the book of Ruth attempts to regain some of that pain associated with Bethlehem. But that pain continues on when the famous David who came from this town rescued his parents from there because he thought they might be held hostage by his enemy Saul (1 Samuel 23). If a town's reputation is shaped by its history, then little Bethlehem could be said to have a sordid reputation. While the Father could have chosen Jerusalem or Bethel for His Son to be born in, the Messiah was born in a town filled with secrets and a painful history.

The ultimate message of Micah 5:2, however, lies not in its history but in its future: "From you One will go forth for Me to be ruler in Israel. His goings forth are from long ago, From the days of eternity." The Lord says that this one will go forth for [or from] Me, that is to do His work and will. The role of this coming one will be as a "ruler." This of course recalls the fact that Saul anointed David in Bethlehem to be the next legitimate ruler of Israel (1 Samuel 16). Ancient scribes affirmed that this is a prophecy about the Messiah, and they told this to the Magi who were hunting for Him (Matt 2:4–6). The common people affirmed this as well (John 7:41–42) although some thought that Jesus could not be that promised one because He came from Galilee, not knowing that His parents moved with Him from Bethlehem to Galilee while He was still a small Child (Matt 2). Jewish commentators have affirmed that ancient Jews interpreted Micah 5:2 as prophesying about the "Messianic King" (S. Goldman, *The Twelve Prophets* [Soncino Books of the Bible, 1957], 174).

And yet the most amazing characteristic of this Promised One ends the verse. "His goings forth are from long ago, from the days of eternity." The word "goings forth" comes from the same root as the earlier word "go forth." This refers to His activities before He "showed up" in Bethlehem, describing His activities and ministries, not His "origin." The word "eternity" is the same word used for Yahweh in Psalms 90:2 and 93:2 as well as in Habakkuk 1:12. The promise could be paraphrased in the following way. The Shepherd King came from Bethlehem in time, but beyond time He came from eternity! The passage culminates with another reference to exile and suffering (Mic 5:3–4) until it concludes, "This one will be the peace" (5:5). This simple statement affirms that Micah is prophesying of the same One whom his "city cousin," Isaiah, described as the "Prince of Peace" (9:6).

Sharp readers of this chapter, however, will remember that I have not answered the rabbi's response to me mentioned in the introduction to this chapter. When I mentioned to him that the Jewish prophet Micah prophesied that Messiah would be born in Bethlehem and Jesus was born there as the fulfillment, he had a quick response: "That refers to David." While I could have mentioned that these words describe a supernatural person who could not be David, I quickly recalled some very basic chronological facts about the timing of David and Micah. You see David lived and died 250 years before Micah's prophecy about a future Messianic King! If it was a prophecy delivered long after David, it could not refer to him! I will never forget that rabbi's quick response. He simply said, "Well it must have meant something to the people in those days, even though we don't know what it means today." My heart was filled with both joy and sadness as I drove home with my wife that night. Joy at the opportunity I had to speak to so many Jewish people but sadness over a Jewish rabbi who could not face the implication of a Jewish prophet's prophecy about his Messiah.

Yes, Bethlehem had a rocky history marked by pain, sordid behavior, danger, and sorrow. But on a night long ago, the House of Bread produced the Bread of Life, and the world has never been the same after that.

───────▼───────

 O Father of the Lord Jesus, our Messiah, the God of glory, may You grant us the spirit of wisdom and revelation in the knowledge of Jesus, that the eyes of our understanding being enlightened, we may know what is the hope of His calling, what are the riches of the glory of His inheritance in the saints, and what is the exceeding greatness of His power toward us who believe, according to the working of His mighty power which He worked in the Messiah when He raised Him from the dead and seated Him at Your right hand in the heavenly realms, far above all principality and power and might and dominion, and every name that is named, not only in this age but also in that which is to come. And You have put all things under His feet, and placed Him as head over all things to the church, which is His body, the fullness of Him who fills all in all. Amen.

(Adapted from Eph 1:17–23)

CHAPTER 6

A King before the KING

When Bible readers move from the Old to the New Testament, they encounter many new ideas and institutions. They encounter groups like the Pharisees, Sadducees, Herodians, and Zealots, who are not mentioned in the Old Testament. New organizations like the synagogue and the Sanhedrin are prominent in the Gospels but do not appear in the Hebrew Scriptures. The last book of the Old Testament, Malachi, was written during a period when the Persians controlled Judea, but early in Matthew's Gospel we read of Roman soldiers, centurions, and procurators. Obviously, something happened to change many of the conditions that existed among the Jewish people at the end of the Old Testament period.

Approximately four hundred years elapsed between the Testaments. These times have been referred to by a number of catchy phrases like "From Malachi to Matthew" and "From Babylon to Bethlehem." Scholars call this period the "Second Temple Period" or "Intertestamental Period." Armies marched across Judea during these tumultuous times, new ideas spread through the land, and new groups and institutions arose to meet the challenges of the day. One of the biggest changes was in language. The Old Testament was written in Hebrew, while the New Testament was written in Greek. The coming of the Greeks during this Intertestamental Period not only altered the language and lifestyle of most Jews but changed the history of the world.

This story begins with the childhood of a remarkable young prince, Alexander, son of Philip of Macedon. Tutored by the philosopher Aristotle, young Alexander showed exceptional physical prowess as a youth, foreshadowing the astounding military career that lay before him. For example, he tamed a wild horse that no one else could handle, named him Bucephalos, and rode him throughout most of his later conquests. His father had conquered and united the Greek peninsula, and, after his death, the youthful Alexander began his amazing career of military conquests. He vowed to avenge the attacks of the Persians that had occurred over a hundred years before, when Xerxes had dared to enter the Greek homeland. Imbued by Greek culture, he desired to spread those Hellenistic ideas along with his conquests. He fulfilled those goals in a career of a dozen years, which altered the history of the Middle East and profoundly affected the life of the Jewish people. He is one of the few individuals in history always mentioned with the title "the Great" following his name, and he justly deserved that designation, although his greatness was measured in other ways than morality!

In 333 BC, Alexander began to exact his revenge when he and his army decisively defeated the Persians in a major battle at Issus in Syria, with Darius the king barely escaping. Following this victory, Alexander entered the Middle East and began to take note of that particular people, the Jews. He requested their help in his battles along the Mediterranean coastline, but they refused, citing their loyalty to the Persians who had allowed them great freedom since the days of Cyrus, the king who permitted them to return from the Babylonian captivity (see Ezra 1:1–4). Josephus, a first-century Jewish historian, vividly described Alexander's exploits at this time, including his siege and conquest of the island fortress of Tyre, forever thereafter connected to the mainland by the causeway he built to enable his troops to reach it.

Bible readers should be particularly interested in this coastal conquest, because the Prophet Zechariah described it in poetic detail in chapter 9, verses 1 to 7 of his book. He predicted Alexander's conquest of Syria (vv. 1–2a), Phoenicia (vv.2b–4), and Philistia (vv. 5–7). At this point, Zechariah prophesied that Alexander would turn his attention to the Jews of Jerusalem: "Then I will encamp at My house as a guard, so that none shall march to and fro; no oppressor shall again march over them, for now I see with My own eyes" (Zech 9:8). In other words, God would deliver them from Alexander's anger. The way this was accomplished is described in a truly fascinating account preserved by Josephus:

> When Jaddua, the high priest, heard that Alexander was coming, he was terrified and ordered his people to join him in prayer and sacrifice to God. When he learned that Alexander was not far from the city of Jerusalem, he went out in procession with the priests and the people. Alexander saw the procession coming toward him: the priests were clothed in linen and the high priest in a robe of blue and gold. On his head was a miter with the golden plate on which God's name was inscribed. Approaching alone, Alexander prostrated himself before the Name and greeted the high priest. As the Jews welcomed Alexander with one voice, his officers wondered if he had suddenly become insane. He replied, "When I was in Macedonia, considering how I could become master of Asia, I saw this very person in my sleep, dressed as he is now. He urged me not to delay, but to cross over confidently and take dominion over the Persians." Alexander was escorted into Jerusalem by the high priest and his attendants. He went up into the temple, where he sacrificed to God according to the high priest's directions. And when the Book of Daniel was shown to him, which predicted that one of the Greeks would destroy the Persian Empire, he thought himself

to be the one so designated. When he offered the Jews whatever they desired, the high priest asked that they might observe their own laws and be exempt from the tribute every
seventh year. Alexander granted these requests" (Whiston
translation, *Antiquities*, Book XI.5).

The passage shown to Alexander was undoubtedly Daniel 8:3–7:

> I raised my eyes and saw, and behold, a ram standing on the
> bank of the canal. It had two horns, and both horns were
> high, but one was higher than the other, and the higher one
> came up last. I saw the ram charging westward and north
> ward and southward. No beast could stand before him, and
> there was no one who could rescue from his power. He did as
> he pleased and became great. As I was considering, behold, a
> male goat came from the west across the face of the whole
> earth, without touching the ground. And the goat had a con
> spicuous horn between his eyes. He came to the ram with the
> two horns, which I had seen standing on the bank of the ca
> nal, and he ran at him in his powerful wrath. I saw him come
> close to the ram, and he was enraged against him and struck
> the ram and broke his two horns. And the ram had no power
> to stand before him, but he cast him down to the ground and
> trampled on him. And there was no one who could rescue
> the ram from his power.

According to Daniel's prophecy, Alexander the Great was the
"male goat . . . from the west" who would decisively conquer the
"ram"; that is, the Persian King Darius. After he spared Jerusalem,
Alexander continued his trek eastward and accomplished just
what Daniel said he would. He completely routed the Persians at
Guagemela in 331 BC and soon had occupied Babylon, Susa, Persepolis, and all the other Persian cities. He continued his conquests

through what we know today as Iran, Pakistan, and Afghanistan, until India eventually lay at his feet. Only the exhaustion and the resistance of his own troops forced him to finally call an end to his campaigns. He finally returned to Babylon, where he lived in oriental splendor until his death in a drunken stupor at the young age of 33.

Following his death, Alexander's great empire was divided among his four generals. Daniel 8:8 foretold this development as well: "Then the goat became exceedingly great, but when he was strong, the great horn was broken, and instead of it there came up four conspicuous horns toward the four winds of heaven." These successors continued his policy of Hellenization, spreading the Greek culture, language, and religion as they founded many cities in the following years. The two divisions of the empire that affected the Jewish people the most in subsequent years were the Seleucids in Syria and the Ptolemies in Egypt. Actually, for a long while, little Judea was something of a bouncing ball going back and forth between these two Greek kingdoms. For approximately one hundred years, the Jews were ruled by the Egyptian Ptolemies, who were generally tolerant and allowed the high priest to freely administer the law to his Jewish subjects.

From about 200 BC onward, however, the Syrian Seleucids began a policy of forced Hellenization that resulted in many young Jewish men becoming enamored with Greek ways and beliefs. Those who remained faithful to the God of their forefathers became known as the Hasidim—the pious ones—who were the forerunners of the Pharisees in New Testament times. This forced Hellenization came to a head with the persecutions of the notorious Antiochus Epiphanes, who sought to force the Jewish people to worship Zeus and defiled the Temple by sacrificing a pig on the altar in 168 BC. This act, of course, led to the period of the Maccabean uprising, described by Josephus and the apocryphal books of the Maccabees. These brave men are those described by Daniel: "but the people who know their God shall stand firm and take action" (Dan 11:32). Their bravery led to the liberation of the Jewish people and the founding of the festival of Hanukkah in December of 165 BC.

While pagan Greek influence was resisted by the faithful during this period, the spread of the Greek language throughout the region could not be halted. Most Jews had learned Greek by the time of the New Testament period. If they were involved in any sort of contact with the outside world, they had to know Greek because it had become the language of international trade. One evidence of the spread of the Greek language can be seen in the very first translation of the Bible, completed during this period. It came to be known as the Septuagint (or the LXX) since it was originally translated by approximately 70 Jewish scholars. The need for such a translation had become acute, especially for Jews living outside the land of Israel (i.e., in the Diaspora), who did not know the Hebrew language well or at all. The Pentateuch was finished around 250 BC, while the rest of the Hebrew Scriptures were certainly finished by AD 1. It was later used by most New Testament authors, who cited it in their quotations of the Old Testament. It also became the "Bible" of the Greek-speaking early church.

While the spread of the Greek language and culture during this time had some negative effects, this development must also be viewed as part of the providential preparation by the Lord for the spread of the gospel message. By the first century, there was, in a real sense, a universal language spoken and/or understood virtually everywhere. The apostles used that language to take the gospel message to the corners of the empire. Also, the written documents comprising the New Testament (with the possible exception of Matthew) were all written in Greek. Actually, these writings were composed in a common form of that language, the Koine Greek, not in the formal classical Greek, known only to scholars. Alexander would have been surprised to know that his spread of Hellenism had actually paved the way for a message that would eventually destroy his beloved Greek gods.

I mentioned earlier that Alexander's conquests in the Middle East were prophesied in outline through the prophet Zechariah (9:1–8). Having recognized that background and fulfillment, how much more powerful is it to read Zechariah 9:9: "Rejoice greatly, O daughter of Zion! Shout in triumph, O daughter of Jerusalem! Behold, your king is coming to you. He is just and endowed with salvation, humble, and mounted on a donkey, even on a colt, the foal of a donkey." A king rode on a mighty stallion; THE KING rode on a donkey. A king struck fear in hearts; THE KING brought joy to hearts. A king brought destruction; THE KING brought salvation. A king was arrogant; THE KING was humble. A dramatic comparison between the two? Very much so! A dramatic contrast between the two? Utterly amazing! Although he was great in his contribution to history, Alexander's contributions were overshadowed by another who died at about the same age that he had died. His kingdom, unlike Alexander's however, did not fall apart after His death. The Messiah's Kingdom continued to attract followers, not by the power of the sword, but by the power of the Word. His life and death still inspire His followers down unto today.

Years ago I was struck by the simple eloquence of the following poem. The author has powerfully compared and contrasted these two individuals, Alexander and Jesus, who each left his respective mark on history, albeit in vastly different ways. Turn this poem into your prayer!

———————▼———————

The Conquerors

Jesus and Alexander died at thirty-three,
One lived and died for self; One died for you and me.
The Greek died on a throne; the Jew died on a cross;
One's life a triumph seemed; the other but a loss.

One led vast armies forth; the other walked alone,
One shed a whole world's blood; the other gave His own.
One won the world in life and lost it all in death;
The other lost His life to win the whole world's faith.

Jesus and Alexander died at thirty-three,
One died in Babylon, and One on Calvary.
One gained all for himself; and One himself He gave.
One conquered every throne; the other every grave.

The one made himself a god, Our God made himself less.
The one lived but to blast, the other but to bless.
When died the Greek, forever fell the throne of swords;
But Jesus died to live, forever Lord of Lords.

Jesus and Alexander died at thirty-three,
The Greek made men slaves, The Jew made men free.
One built a throne on blood; the other built on love.
The one was born of earth; the other from above.

One won all of this earth, to lose all earth and heaven.
The other gave up all, that all to Him be given.
The Greek forever died; the Jew forever lives.
He loses all who gets, and wins all things who gives.

Charles Ross Weede

CHAPTER 7

A Not so Silent Night

I wish I could tell you that I came up with this chapter title, which turns on its head one of the most familiar Christmas carol titles, "Silent Night." I actually borrowed it from a stimulating book by Verlyn Verbrugge titled *A Not So Silent Night* (Kregel, 2009). In this little book, the author attempts to uncover what he calls "the dark side of Christmas," a side that is marked by pain, humiliation, fear, and danger. These negative words are not usually associated with the joy and light that mark our Christmas celebrations. The author is not really trying to be a modern "Scrooge" who throws a cold blanket on our season of joy, but he argues that these darker elements actually convey the meaning of the Advent and cause it to shine even brighter against the dark background of the culture in the first-century Roman and Jewish worlds. Until we shed tears with Mary and Joseph and appreciate the war on the horizon, we will never fully understand the awesome character of what happened in that little town of Bethlehem. In this chapter we take a fresh look at Luke 2 and those shepherds and angels. We also look again at what could be called the very first Christmas carol.

Before we look further at those shepherds, however, we need to revisit the specific place they visited on the first nativity night.

Most Bible versions render Luke 2:7 as follows: "And she gave birth to her firstborn son; and she wrapped Him in cloths, and laid Him in a manger, because there was no room for them in the *inn*" (NASB). We read this word I have italicized as an ancient equivalent of a hotel. Now if we have seen this play once, we have seen it a dozen times. Joseph and his heavily pregnant wife are at the door of an inn when the grouchy, heartless innkeeper slams his door in their faces with the infamous two words: "No room!" Is that the picture we should envision?

While there was the equivalent of an inn in ancient times, and we will see one in the New Testament, perhaps we need to revisit this image in light of the ancient practice of lodging strangers and what the original language really conveys. Joseph is headed to the home of his ancestors and presumably he had relatives living there. Other New Testament references seem to imply that physical and spiritual relatives lodged with those "kinfolk" as they travelled (Gal 6:10; 1 Pet 4:9; 3 John 8). This is precisely the implication of Luke 2:7 with the word that has often been translated "inn." This Greek word (*kataluma*) occurs only two other times in the New Testament and in those times, it is not an "inn" but a "guest room." Jesus asked Peter and John to locate one and make it ready for Him and His disciples to observe the Passover (Mark 14:14 and Luke 22:11). The *kataluma* was undoubtedly a room in a person's home—one that was probably not in general use except for special occasions to welcome a guest. The authoritative Greek dictionary that students refer to as "BDAG" says this word is "best understood here as a lodging or guest room, with the context permitting the sense of a dining room as well" (521).

What makes this point even stronger is that there is a perfectly good word for what we think of as an "inn" (*pandocheion*), and it is even used by Luke in his same book. It is the "inn" to which the "Good Samaritan" took the wounded man and where he paid the innkeeper for the lodging (Luke 10:34). So that night in Bethlehem, we should envision a relative's home that was already filled with visiting relatives who were there for the census. The only "room" was on the first floor, the traditional place for the animals to be kept. While we don't know the details, some may think the relatives quite heartless for not making room for this pregnant "cousin." Again, while we can't be dogmatic, perhaps word had spread about her questionable pregnancy and they did not want to seemingly approve of her shame by making room for her even in the guest room. Whatever be the dynamics, Mary and Joseph find themselves among some animals for the evening. Perhaps this is an early foretaste of what Isaiah 53 said about the Servant being despised and rejected and not esteemed (Isaiah 53). One is also reminded of John 1:11: "He came unto His own and His own did not receive Him." Evidently such rejection did not wait to begin later at the Passion week!

While Luke 2 begins with the Holy Family in spare quarters in Bethlehem, it continues with a group of shepherds in the fields outside Bethlehem plus an angel appearing to them and announcing some really great news (Luke 2:13–14). The announcement is expanded by some very special singing. Our Christmas carols reflect this scene quite vividly.

- "Sing, choirs of angels, sing in exultation…"
- "Angels we have heard on high, sweetly singing o'er the plains."
- "…from angels bending near the earth to touch their harps of gold" (from "It Came upon the Midnight Clear")

As moving as are these hymnal melodies, it is actually hard to find them embedded in the text of Luke 2. Then what IS there you ask? At this point I am actually afraid that what I am about to write is going to convince some readers that I am that "Christmas Scrooge" trying to destroy the joy of Christmas celebrations. I assure you that I enjoy our holiday gatherings and especially my family's gathering around the tree as much as anyone. Hear me out when I say that I am not against those songs above, but I just want you to notice that there is another side to this "Not So Silent Night." And that "other side" is that the host of heaven has gathered, not just for a joyous announcement, but for war!

For some of what follows, I am indebted to the Verbrugge book I mentioned at the beginning of this chapter. Just try to follow our argument and see if it makes sense, because I think it is Biblically and theologically sound. The first matter to consider is the mental image that we have of angels. The biblical word cherubim has morphed into the English word cherub, which evokes images of fat and cute little creatures that are intended to warm our hearts. Let it be said clearly that such images are absolutely foreign to the Biblical description of angelic beings. The second matter is the Hebrew term *tsva*, which is often used to describe a group of angels and is translated into English as "host." But *tsva* is better understood as a military term. In fact, even today in Modern Hebrew, *tsva* means "army." At the age of eighteen, every Israeli goes to the *tsva*, the army.

Now the New Testament is written in Greek. When Luke refers to these angels gathered together, he uses the Greek word **stratia**, which is the word used to translate the Hebrew **tsva** ("army") in the ancient Greek Old Testament. "And suddenly there appeared with the angel a multitude of the heavenly **host** (**stratia**) praising God and saying" (Luke 2:13, NASB). The New English Translation is bold enough to render it as follows: "Suddenly a vast, heavenly **army** appeared with the angel, praising God and saying…" Why would they do that? A survey of the Old Testament uses of this word clearly answers that question.

In classical Greek, the word is used almost exclusively in a military sense for an army or group of soldiers. In the ancient Greek Old Testament, it is used nineteen times for human armies:

sometimes Egyptian (Exod 14:4, 9, 17), sometimes Assyrian (2 Chron 32:9), and often for Israel's armies (Num 10:28; Deut 20:9; 2 Sam 3:23; 18:16). The other nine uses of *stratia* refer to nonmaterial "hosts" as is the case in Luke 2:13. All nine of these uses are linked with the word "heavenly." Admittedly, sometimes the "host" may refer to the stars (2 Chron 33:3, 5). In at least two of these verses, the "host of heaven" refers to spiritual beings who are on the Lord's side of the battle (1 Kings 22:19; Neh 9:6). In two passages, it appears that heavenly beings, i.e. angels, form an army to oppose the pagan enemies. Second Kings 6:17 says that the hills are full of horses and chariots of fire around Elisha, which become visible at his command. Judges 5:20 describes the stars as fighting against Sisera, obviously referring to spiritual beings who fought for God's people against overwhelming human odds.

Now how does this all relate to the heavenly host in Luke 2? As contradictory as it may sound to Christmas being a time of peace (we will mention that later), the Advent included the assembling of the heavenly host for a war, one that would be fought in spiritual fields, not earthly ones. Jesus came to destroy the works of the Devil (1 John 3:8), and Satan reciprocated with his own spiritual assaults on Jesus. Jesus fought with demonic forces in Mark 5:1–20 when they did not want to give up their ownership of the Gerasene. It is significant that they called their name "legion" which is also the name for a Roman military division of six thousand soldiers (Mark 5:9). In the Garden, He acknowledged that He had a spiritual army ready to be called to active duty: "Or do you think that I cannot appeal to My Father, and He will at once put at My disposal more than twelve legions of angels?" (Matt 26:53). In other words, Satan had his legions and Jesus had His legions. Is it a stretch to think that the legions of angels ready to do the bidding of their Commander in Matthew 26 are identical to the legions of the heavenly host (*stratia*) that evening outside Bethlehem? To borrow a modern expression, I think that the song sung to the shepherds the night of Jesus' birth was the celestial version of "Hail to the Chief." In other words, that so-called "Silent Night" was the beginning of war!

But what of those oft-quoted words of the heavenly carol: "Peace on earth. Good will to men?" These verbless expressions were not a pronouncement like they sound in the KJV; they were a wish or a prayer like the many of these salutations in the New Testament letters: "May peace and grace be yours." Furthermore, there is strong evidence that the expression should be read as in earlier Greek manuscripts, "Glory to God in the highest, and on earth peace among men with whom He is pleased" (Luke 2:14). The last word in the earliest readings is referring to the Divine good pleasure that rests on those who have accepted His rule and have ceased to fight against Him! The same word is used in that sense in Eph 1:5, 9 (NKJV) and was used by Jesus in Luke 10:21: "Yes, Father, for this way was *well-pleasing* in Your sight." The peace of Luke 2:14 is not a generic prayer for disarmament in international relations. It is a prayer that God's people may experience true *shalom* (peace) in their relationship with God. That peace is for those on whom His favor rests.

While there is nothing wrong about wishing for international peace between nations, this is not the peace that this heavenly army was singing about. This peace is for believers who "have been justified by faith and have peace with God through our Lord Jesus Christ" (Rom 5:1). That is the message from this "not so silent night" long ago that is so needed to be shouted out loudly for today's world!

For this reason I bow my knees to the Father of His messiah, our Lord Jesus, from whom the whole family in heaven and earth is named, that You would grant us, according to the riches of Your glory, to be strengthened with might through His Spirit in the inner man, that Messiah may dwell in our hearts through faith; so that we being rooted and grounded in love, may be able to comprehend with all the saints what *is* the width and length and depth and height--to know the love of our Messiah which passes knowledge; that we may be filled with all the fullness of God. Now to Him who is able to do exceedingly abundantly above all that we ask or think, according to the power that works in us, to Him *be* glory in the church by Messiah Jesus to all generations, forever and ever. Amen.

(Adapted from Eph 3:14-21)

CHAPTER 8

A Christmas for Old People

I t is one of my favorite places in the Land of Israel to visit with a group, and I have had the privilege to lead over fifty groups to this exciting site! The excavations since 1967 of the area south of the ancient Temple Mount have uncovered the monumental staircase that Jewish pilgrims and locals would ascend to enter the Huldah Gate into the upper level of the Temple Mount. Of course, that Temple was destroyed in AD 70 and that staircase was covered by rubble and stones for over nineteen hundred years. The staircase is remarkably well-preserved, and I usually have my students sitting on it as I point out the surrounding features. From that vantage point we can look over at the Jewish tombs on the Mount of Olives, some of which can still be seen today. If Jesus taught on these steps, He could point out those whitewashed tombs full of dead men's bones and compare them to the hypocritical religious leaders who lacked any true inner spirituality. Embedded in that wide staircase are the remains of *mikvaot*, Jewish ritual baths, not mentioned in the Old Testament but developed later for ritual immersions to purify women after giving birth to a child. I am also eager then to point out some important events in Luke 2 that undoubtedly took place exactly in this strategic area.

Let us explain some Old Testament background information that can illuminate some important but sometimes overlooked passages in the account of the infant days of Messiah Jesus. As was mentioned, two important events are located here concerning a young Jewish lad born to a Jewish mother. First was her purification after the birth of a child. When any secretion would emerge from a woman, it made her ritually unclean until she immersed herself in a *mikveh*. This took place forty days following the birth of a male child and eighty days after the birth of a female child (Lev 12:1–5). Of course there was another important ceremony for a Jewish son: his circumcision, which was to take place on the eighth day after his birth. The ritual of circumcision, however, was not performed in the Temple but was done in the home and for Jesus this would have taken place in Bethlehem. So Mary would have immersed herself in one of those *mikvaot*, over three dozen of which have been discovered to the south and west of the Temple Mount, which would be convenient for pilgrims to use before they entered the Temple.

The other important ceremony for a Jewish boy, and one still performed today, is the *pidyon haben*, literally the "redemption of the first-born son." This act was commanded in Numbers 3:40–51 and requires a little more Old Testament explanation for non-Jewish readers. This background will allow us to appreciate the events in Luke 2, which involved two senior citizens in the Temple on the day when Joseph and Mary showed up with a forty-day-old son in their arms. In the earliest Old Testament period, the oldest son was set aside to be the priest for the family. This did not mean that he did not work a "regular job" but that he had an honored role to represent the family in religious matters. When things went bad at the foot of Mount Sinai while Moses tarried on the mountain, it appeared that the entire nation had gone apostate in what has been called the "golden calf apostasy" (Exodus 32). Moses came down the mountain and saw that the people "were out of control" (32:25). In righteous anger he laid down an invitation to anyone who was for Yahweh to come and help him punish the idolaters. Sadly, only those from the tribe of Levi joined him, and they helped Moses punish the idolaters. As a reward for their faithfulness in this time of maximum apostasy, the Levites were rewarded by a special dedication to the Lord (32:27–29). We must wait until the legislation in the Book of Numbers to learn how that tribe of Levi was eventually rewarded for their faithfulness. The Levites actually replaced the firstborn sons as the priests in Israel (Num 3:5–13). A ceremony was then established in which the firstborn of every family had to be "redeemed" or bought back from being a priest because a whole tribe was now providing the priests (Num 3:49–51).

This is the exact ceremony that awaited the firstborn son of Mary that day in the Temple! He had to be "redeemed" or bought back from being an earthly priest. The parents would find an available priest in the Temple and place their son in his arms. Then they would give the priest five coins and the priest would give the firstborn son back to the parents; thus the son had been "redeemed" or bought back from a priest! If all of this sounds odd and strange, I want to tell you that Jewish parents who are not Levites (who are the only ones who know what tribe they are from!) perform this ceremony today for every son that opens his mother's womb. If you are wondering if this could be a profitable operation for Jewish men who are *Cohanim* (priests), the man receiving the coins is supposed to give them to charity. This is the very ceremony that awaited the firstborn son Jesus and His parents that day in the Temple. After her immersion in the *mikveh*, Mary and Joseph ascended that staircase, entered the Huldah Gate, made their way further up the staircase in an underground passage, and then emerged into the sunlight of the massive courtyard of the Temple. There they would begin looking for the first available Levitical priest so they could perform this required ritual.

Now there enters into this drama an old man and eventually an old woman. Luke seems to develop a theme in his first two chapters about Senior Saints. In chapter one, the elderly couple Zechariah and Elizabeth received the wonderful news that their barrenness was over! The miraculous conception, birth, and circumcision of the Messianic forerunner is then powerfully played out before us (Luke 1:5–25). That special child came to be called John the Baptist. Now Luke describes for us another moving scene involving two more senior saints. Simeon is described as a pious priest who was daily looking for the Messiah's arrival. The Lord had even assured him that he would not die before he had seen with his own eyes the Lord's promised servant (2:25–26).

The drama that played out very quietly between this couple, the old man, and the forty-day-old boy, although probably not noticed by many present, was fraught with pathos and great feeling. Think of the aged Simeon coming every day to the Temple, knowing that the Lord had promised that he would live to see the Messiah. As he aged and the inevitable end was drawing near, he could be excused if he wondered if that day would ever arrive. As he entered the crowded court, I can imagine the Lord tapping him on the shoulder and telling him, "Simeon, there He is!" His glance catches the eyes of the couple, so they approach and hand the infant Jesus into his arms. The ceremony of the coins and the "redemption" was not the most important thing at this point as he looked up to heaven and with thanksgiving in his heart and trembling in his hands he lifts up the baby toward heaven. Let us now hear his own words: "Now Lord, You are releasing Your bond-servant to depart in peace, according to Your word; for my eyes have seen Your salvation, which You have prepared in the presence of all peoples, a light of revelation to the Gentiles, and the glory of Your people Israel" (2:29–32).

What a way to go! I don't know if these were his last words, but they certainly would have been the greatest words of his

long life. The last words about a revelation for the Gentiles are a
clear reference to some wonderful promises in Isaiah such as
9:2; 42:6; and 49:6. The "glory" of Israel could only mean one
thing: this little one was the Lord's Anointed One, the Messiah.
I have often wondered what the young mother must have wondered as this old man said such things about her little one.
Maybe she wondered: "Well, Lord, You told me that He would
be the long-awaited Promised One for my people, Israel, but
did I just hear that He will bring light also to the Gentiles?
There is more to this than I ever imagined!" I conclude this because of what the next verse says about their reaction. "And His
father and mother were amazed at the things which were being
said about Him" (2:33).

If this encounter ended there, it would have been enough, but
when old Simeon handed the Child back to His parents, he delivered a final word that must have tempered their wonder with
some real pain. And Simeon blessed them and said to Mary His
mother, "Behold, this *Child* is appointed for the fall and rise of
many in Israel, and for a sign to be opposed—and a sword will
pierce even your own soul—to the end that thoughts from many
hearts may be revealed" (2:34–35). Oh, why do his joyful words
have to end on that painful note? What does it mean that a sword
will someday cut into her soul? It would be over three decades
before she would know exactly what they meant. As she stood
before a Roman cross looking at the broken body of her Son, she
would experience the pain in her soul that would be the counter-
point of the joy that must have flooded her soul on this day in the
Temple. Before the Messiah's glory must come His suffering, so
graphically described in such passages as Isaiah 53 and later described by Peter (1 Pet 1:10–11).

But as these words began to sink in, another senior saint approached. It was a woman who bore the name of an Old Testament saint who must have also cherished the few days she had

with her young "son of the promise" before she returned him to the tabernacle/temple of her day (1 Samuel 1–2). Like her OT counterpart, her Hebrew name was Hannah, but Luke calls her by the shorter Greek equivalent, Anna. Let his words graphically describe the touching encounter.

> "And there was a prophetess, Anna the daughter of Phanuel, of the tribe of Asher. She was advanced in years and had lived with *her* husband seven years after her marriage, and then as a widow to the age of eighty-four. She never left the temple, serving night and day with fastings and prayers. At that very moment she came up and *began* giving thanks to God and continued to speak of Him to all those who were looking for the redemption of Jerusalem" (Luke 2:36–38).

Two senior saints are seen here finishing their course by beholding the One who would eventually bring glory and redemption to their people. It is a beautiful irony that the little child who was "redeemed" physically from the hands of the old priest Simeon should be announced by the old Anna as the one who would spiritually "redeem" Jerusalem from her heavy burdens!

Yes, in a very real way we say that "Christmas is for kids." It is such a delight to see them receiving and sharing presents on Christmas morning. It is also a joy to watch their wonder at hearing the old story of Jesus' birth and imagine that they could be one of those shepherds near the manger. But in this story, which is also an important part of Luke's "Advent" account, two senior saints find the greatest gift of their long lives. Yes, this day was surely "A Christmas for Old People."

Lord, I do not cease to pray and to ask that I may be filled with the knowledge of Your will in all wisdom and spiritual understanding, that I may walk worthy of the Lord, fully pleasing Him, being fruitful in every good work and increasing in the knowledge of God. May I be strengthened with all might, according to Your glorious power, for all patience and longsuffering with joy, giving thanks to You, Father, who has qualified us to be partakers of the inheritance of the saints in the light. You have delivered me from the power of darkness and replanted me in the kingdom of Your Beloved Son, in Whom I have redemption through His blood, the forgiveness of sins.

(Adapted from Col 1:9–14)

CHAPTER 9

A Great Herod?

A king named Herod loomed large in the Nativity account of Matthew (2:1–12). He is to be distinguished from his son Herod Antipas, who also would face Jesus during the Passion Week (Luke 23:8–12). History has bestowed upon the original Herod the descriptive title, "the Great." He is one of a handful of persons (Alexander, Catherine, Peter) whose name is always accompanied by that adjective. The primary Jewish chronicler of his period, Josephus, was the first to use the actual phrase "Herod the Great" in his *Antiquities of the Jews.* He used the phrase, however, not to describe the "greatness" of Herod, but to distinguish Herod from his sons and grandsons of the same name. In other words, he used the title in the sense of "the greater" or "the older." Whatever the original reason, the name has stuck on the one who ruled from Jerusalem as the "king of the Jews" from 37 to 4 BC.

Although Herod died soon after Jesus' birth, his shadow continued to loom over the New Testament through his huge building projects and through his descendants, who continued to rule over the Jewish people in Israel throughout the first century AD. We could question whether Herod deserved to have "the Great" added to his name. As we shall see, his personal and family life was such that he deserved more the title of "Herod the Terrible." On the other hand, he certainly left a "great" mark on history and well deserves the three books it took Josephus to describe his life and exploits (*Antiquities*, XIV.15–17).

Herod's Background

Herod was not born of direct Israelite ancestry. Josephus calls him an "Idumean," the Roman term for the descendants of the Old Testament Edomites, who dwelt in the mountainous region below the Dead Sea. Around 128 BC, John Hyrcanus, a zealous Hasmonean Jewish king, conquered the Idumeans and forcibly converted them to Judaism. Herod's forebears, probably his grandparents, evidently were among those forced converts.

Josephus once called Herod a "half-Jew" (*Antiquities*, XIV.15.2), indicating not only his ancestry but possibly his half-hearted identification with the Jewish people. One church father also mentioned that Herod's father was from Ashkelon in Philistia and had been carried off to Idumea, where he had grown up as one of them. Therefore, it seems that Herod had a mixed Philistine-Edomite background while also identifying outwardly with Judaism as a descendant of forced converts.

His father, Antipater, had become a supporter of the new Roman rulers following their conquest of the Middle East in 63 BC. As the appointed governor of Judea, Antipater maneuvered constantly to ensure a future for his two sons, Phasael and Herod. Antipater and his sons knew that currying the favor of the Romans was the only way to do this. As a young man, Herod built a reputation by creatively apprehending some Jewish brigands in the region of the Galilee where he was serving under his father. He flushed them out of the Arbel caves, where they were hiding, by lowering his men in baskets from the precipitous cliffs above the caves. It was the first of many wily maneuvers that characterized and endeared him to his Roman patrons.

Herod's Rise to Power

After the violent deaths of his father and brother, Herod began his rise to kingship in 40 BC. Antigonus, a descendant of the Hasmonean kings, was pressing for a restoration of that monarchy. Herod desperately needed assistance, so he scurried off to Rome, where he convinced Mark Antony and Octavius (the future Caesar Augustus) that supporting his cause would be in Rome's best interest. He was so convincing that the Senate of Rome conferred on him the title "King of the Jews" in 40 BC.

Three years later, Herod became king in fact as well as in name. Antigonus was executed by the Romans, and Herod began his bloody rule by executing forty-five wealthy and prominent supporters of the Hasmoneans. Herod had finally arrived, but his new position was one that he constantly had to protect by a combination of guile and brutality.

Herod's Accomplishments

Herod indeed committed some monstrous acts. Because of those foul deeds, it is easy to overlook his truly amazing accomplishments. Although experiencing constant conflict within his own household, he maintained the outward peace of the nation remarkably well. His kingdom expanded to the boundaries it had known during the reign of Solomon, the days of its most distant frontiers.

It is in the area of his vast building projects that Herod left a legacy for all to behold, even until today. He took a sleepy little fishing port on the Mediterranean coast called Strato's Tower and transformed it into a major port and mercantile center. He renamed it Caesarea after his patron, Emperor Caesar Augustus. He also adorned the Old Testament city of Samaria with equally magnificent architecture and called it Sebaste, the Greek word for Augustus.

It was in Jerusalem, however, that Herod left his most magnificent edifices. Next to the western Jaffa Gate of the city he constructed three huge towers that, because of their size and beauty, were left standing by the Romans when they destroyed the city in AD 70. In addition to the towers and next to them, he built his own magnificent palace, which rivaled those of kings and emperors worldwide. A theater, a hippodrome, an aqueduct, a fortress named for Mark Antony—the list goes on. Remarkably, the huge stones in many of these structures are still visible today, each with his own unique edging which was a signature of his handiwork.

His largest and most significant Jerusalem building project was his reconstruction and vast embellishment of the old Zerubbabel Temple, which had stood for nearly 400 years. Herod spared no expense or effort in this project. He employed and trained priests for the construction of restricted areas so the daily service could continue unabated. He constructed a huge rectangular platform with a perimeter of nearly half a mile, supporting it with huge arches and vaults on the sloping sides of Mount Moriah. Pillars nearly fifty feet high adorned the porticoes, while limestone ashlars weighing sometimes nearly forty tons comprised the 100-foot-high retaining walls. Archaeological labors to the south and west of these walls have revealed magnificent staircases, ritual purification baths, shops, and elaborate water systems. The debris from the AD 70 destruction as well as the "fill" of subsequent ages have been removed to unveil to visitors the astonishing wonder of this biggest and best of all Herod's construction projects. Even the rabbis, who were not always Herod's biggest fans, often remarked, "He who has not seen Herod's Temple has never seen a beautiful building."

Another type of Herodian construction reveals the darker side of the king's character. Throughout Judea, Herod constructed huge fortresses and palaces not only for "getting away from the office" in Jerusalem, but as retreats to which he could flee if rebellion against his autocratic rule ever erupted. Next to a magnificent winter palace in Jericho was the fortress of Cypros, named for his mother. On the other side of the Dead Sea, near his beloved hot springs, he built Machaerus, which, according to Josephus, later became a prison for the condemned John the Baptist. Near Bethlehem, he built an artificial hill with a fortress inside its "cone." This fortress, humbly called the "Herodium," was one of his favorite hangouts and later served as his burial location. On the western shore of the Dead Sea, he surrounded a 1,200-foot-high rock with a wall boasting 72 towers, plus palaces, swimming pools, and huge storehouses—the virtually inaccessible stronghold called Masada. This remote fortress became the last stand of the Zealot warriors against the Romans in AD 73.

Herod's "fortress mentality" is also illustrated by the way he treated those whom he thought had designs on his throne.

Herod's Crimes

It is a strange irony that someone so personally powerful should be so insanely fearful of those around him. No one whom he suspected of treason was safe—not even his family members. Herod married a total of ten wives. In 29 BC, he executed Mariamne, the one he loved most, because of his insane jealousy. His guilty conscience over this act tormented him for the next twenty years. Soon after he came to the throne, Herod ordered the "accidental" drowning of the young high priest, Aristobulus III, because he feared that the Hasmonean teen's potential might lead to an uprising. The harmless 80-year-old Hasmonean priest Hyrcanus II was also executed for the unjustifiable accusation of treason.

The last years of Herod's life were marked by further executions resulting from his extreme paranoia and the intrigues of his vast household. In 7 BC, he strangled Alexander and Aristobulus, the twin sons of Mariamne, on trumped-up charges of treason arising from their jealous court rivals. Again and again he altered his will, alternately including and then excluding some of his many sons. As his illnesses increased and his mental state deteriorated, he executed his son, Antipater, a few days before his death, thus altering his will one final time. When he heard of this last execution, his Roman patron Augustus remarked in a pun even clearer in the Greek: "It is safer to be Herod's pig (*hus*) than Herod's son (*huios*)."

Knowing that there would be certain jubilation in the land at the news of his demise, Herod ordered that hundreds of Jewish leaders be imprisoned in the stadium at Jericho and gave the order that they be executed immediately after he died. This was to ensure that there would be mourning after his death rather than rejoicing. Mercifully, that last order was not carried out.

Herod's Legacy

Herod the Great is mentioned directly in the New Testament only in the account of Jesus' birth in Bethlehem, in conjunction with the visit of the wise men and his subsequent slaughter of the young children (Matt 2:1–16). The "Herod" of the later Gospel accounts was Herod Antipas, his son. The "Herod" in Acts 12 was Agrippa I, his grandson. Josephus did not mention this heinous crime, causing some critics to question the reliability of the account. The event, however, fits perfectly in the context of Herod's mental state and his insane fear that someone would take over his throne. What Matthew briefly narrates appears to be entirely consistent with all that we know of Herod, especially in the tortured last days of his miserable life.

The question from the Magi, "Where is He who has been born King of the Jews?" (Matt 2:2), takes on new significance when we recall that this is the exact title bestowed on Herod by the Roman Senate more than 30 years earlier. Herod had been *made* "king of the Jews"; the Magi were seeking one who had been *born* "King of the Jews." No wonder Herod was eager to meet this "King." He would then do to Him what he had done to his own sons!

Soon after the Messiah's birth and Herod's failure to eliminate Him, the sick and miserable old man finally expired in another of his palaces in Jericho. He was buried following a fifteen-mile royal funeral procession in that fortress mentioned earlier, the Herodium. This artificial, cone-shaped hill stands silently today just a few miles from Bethlehem. As a matter of fact, the soldiers who carried out the murderous crime on the innocent children of that tiny nearby town may have been dispatched from this very fortress. The view from this fortress reaches from the Dead Sea on the east to Jerusalem in the north around to Bethlehem on the west. The whole sad story comes alive as one stands on the top of this imposing fortress. Today one can only imagine its once-glorious beauty. Now it is an empty shell recovered by the archaeologists, who only recently have been able to find Herod's exact burial place. Not surprisingly, the tomb and his royal sarcophagus had been shattered into pieces, probably by later Zealots who also hated him.

Herod's kingdom is no more and it has no continuing influence. The kingdom of Israel's Messiah, however, continues. He who sought to destroy his rival "King of the Jews" is gone. The helpless little infant, however, born under the brooding shadow of that Herodium fortress, is alive and well!

The *king by might* is gone—the *King by right* lives forever!

———————▼———————

O Lord Jesus, You are worthy to take the scroll, and to open its seals, for You were slain, and have redeemed us to God by Your blood out of every tribe and tongue and people and nation. You have also made us kings and priests to our God, and we shall reign on the earth. Worthy are You, the Lamb who was slain, to receive power and riches and wisdom and strength and honor and glory and blessing! Blessing and honor and glory and power be to Yahweh who sits on the throne and to the Lamb, forever and ever!"

(Adapted from Rev 5:9–13)

CHAPTER 10

A Mythology of the Magi

The visit of the Magi to the Child-Messiah, recorded in Matthew 2:1–12, is one of the most familiar Biblical scenes to most Christians. The average conception of this event, however, has been unfortunately marred by a large number of popular misconceptions. Only when we view this passage through historically sensitive, Jewish eyes can we discern the accurate meaning of the Magi's journey to find the one who was born "King of the Jews."

It is amazing to realize how many misconceptions surround these events. Some of these come from the popular song, "We Three Kings of Orient Are." Consider the following list of erroneous ideas about the wise men:

1. They were *three* in number.
2. They were *kings*.
3. They were from the *Orient* (i.e., the Far East).
4. They were named *Caspar, Melchior*, and *Balthazar*.
5. One of them was a *black* man.
6. They visited the baby Jesus *in a stable*.
7. They followed an astronomical comet or *nova* to Bethlehem.

All of these ideas compose what might be called the *mythology of the Magi*. Some of the misconceptions can be corrected by simply reading Matthew 2:1–12. Others can be dispelled by a logical reading of the text, giving attention to its historical and Jewish background.

The idea that there were three kings named Caspar, Melchior, and Balthazar dates from medieval times, as does the idea that one of them was a black man. Matthew does not mention the number of Magi; probably the three different types of gifts ("gold, and frankincense, and myrrh" in 2:11) gave rise to the traditional number of three visitors. Also, they are not called *kings*, but *Magi*, a special caste of religious men in Persia that we will examine later. Matthew 2:1–2 says that they were from "the east." In modern times we might think of lands like the Far East. That is not, however the way the term was used in biblical language. The "east" was that region just beyond the Tigris and Euphrates Rivers, which would be the area of ancient Persia and today's Iran and eastern Iraq. Being from this region, it is unlikely one of them was black, although this is remotely possible if one of them came from as far as India. Their names, of course, are purely traditional.

Far more prevalent is the idea, perpetuated by millions of nativity scenes, that the Magi were present with their camels along with the shepherds at the manger of the baby Jesus. This idea confuses Matthew's version with Luke's account of the nativity, particularly Luke 2:15–20, and is refuted by statements in Matthew 2:1–16. First, we read in Matthew 2:1, "Now after Jesus was born in Bethlehem of Judea in the days of Herod the king, behold, wise men from the east came to Jerusalem." Furthermore, Matthew 2:11 states, "And going into the house [not a stable or cave], they saw the child . . . [*paidion* in Greek, not *brephos*, the word for 'infant' in Luke 2:12, 16]." Jesus could have been as much as two years old, since Herod ordered all the boys from two and under to be killed, according to the time when the star had originally been seen by the Magi (Matt 2:7, 16). Whatever age Jesus was at this time, He was definitely not a baby in a manger. He was a young child living with His parents in Bethlehem before their flight into Egypt and eventual settling in Nazareth (Matt 2:19–23).

According to many interpreters, the Magi were astrologers who had discerned through their stargazing that the sign of a Jewish king had appeared and that He had been born somewhere in Israel. While the Magi may have engaged in some form of astrology, it is difficult to comprehend how God would communicate His will through a means He had so strongly condemned in passages such as Deuteronomy 18:9–14 and Isaiah 47:12–14. If we allow for such a method of Divine communication, how can we condemn the utilization of astrology for fortune telling today?

Others do not emphasize the Magi's astrology but suggest that these men had observed some unique astronomical phenomenon: a comet, a supernova, or a planetary conjunction. For example, the great astronomer Kepler observed in AD 1603 an unusual conjunction of planets and found that in 6 BC there had been an unusual conjunction of Jupiter, Saturn, and Mars. Therefore, Kepler placed the nativity of Jesus at that time. Chinese astronomical tables also testify to the appearance of a comet in 4 BC, agreeing approximately with the date of the birth. Although this explanation has satisfied many sincere students of the Word, it does not explain the fact that the Magi referred to "His star" (Matt 2:2). Furthermore, it is difficult to comprehend how such an astronomical phenomenon could have moved to Bethlehem and how it "went before them until it came to rest over the place where the Child was" (Matt 2:9). If a comet had performed that feat, there would have been no house or town remaining from the heat!

Having evaluated the various myths surrounding these interesting visitors, what can be concluded about their identity and their knowledge about the promised Jewish king? Furthermore, what was the nature of that wondrous "star" which prompted their long journey? It is important to recognize that there is no real necessity to look beyond the sacred Hebrew Scriptures, for the Jewish understanding of Matthew 2:1–11 provides us with all the keys for the passage's explanation.

For example, it is distinctly possible that the prophecies of Balaam served as the source for the expectation of a Jewish king who would be the national deliverer. Of the four oracles delivered by that fascinating man from "Pethor, which is near the River" (Num 22:5, the Euphrates River in the land of Persia), the last is most expressive: "I see him, but not now; I behold him, but not near: a star shall come out of Jacob, and a scepter shall rise out of Israel; it shall crush the forehead of Moab and break down all the sons of Sheth" (Num 24:17). I think that it is probable that the Magi from Persia had preserved the words of their ancestor Balaam and remembered his ancient prophecy when a "Star" appeared out of Jacob.

While the evidence for the above assertion is interesting to consider, an even stronger source for the Magi's knowledge comes from the Book of Daniel. In the Greek Septuagint translation of Daniel 2:2, 10, one of the words translated "wise men" is the same as the Greek word used in Matthew 2 (*magoi*). The function of these Magi in Nebuchadnezzar's Babylon was to serve as a religious caste that served in the state religion. One of their functions was to interpret dreams—a role in which they failed miserably in Daniel 2:1–13 and so were ordered to be killed. Note Daniel 2:13: "So the decree went out, and the wise men were about to be killed; and they sought Daniel and his companions, to kill them." Therefore, Daniel and his three friends were associated with the Magi due to their God-given ability demonstrated earlier in Daniel 1:20–21.

When Daniel accurately interpreted Nebuchadnezzar's dream in Daniel 2:17–45, he was rewarded with an even higher position among them: "Then the king gave Daniel high honors and many great gifts, and made him ruler over the whole province of Babylon and chief prefect over all the wise men of Babylon" (Dan 2:48). With this information, it is proper to remind ourselves of Daniel's amazing prophecy of the "seventy weeks" in Daniel 9:24–27. Among many truths mentioned in that prophecy, verse 26 states that "Messiah (shall) be cut off" after a total period of 69 "sevens" (483 years). Therefore, Daniel's book provides a timetable for the coming of the Messiah. This timetable from their leader must have been kept through the years by the Magi even when Babylon was conquered by the Persians.

There must have been a growing expectancy among the Magi as the years passed by. Even though this prophecy dealt primarily with the Jewish people, these Magi must have been watchful of it since it was originally given through one *of their own* many years before. It should not be forgotten that a large Jewish community continued to exist in Persia and in the city of Babylon down through the centuries, even until the early 1950s. They would have cherished Daniel's prophecies and kept the hope of it alive.

Some have also suggested that one of the functions of the Magi was that of *king-makers*. It was they who went through the ritual of crowning new kings in Babylon and Persia. This would also shed light on their desire to encounter the "King of the Jews" and to "worship Him" (Matt 2:2).

Having seen the Old Testament background of the Magi, what help can be found there for the correct interpretation of the star? Must we consider only an astrological or astronomical explanation? Mention has been previously made of the objections to the idea that the star was seen in astrological observations. Furthermore, the idea that a physical star could stand over Bethlehem is simply incredulous. The supernatural character of this brightness spoken of as "His star" (Matt 2:2) becomes evident. I suggest that this unique shining was that of the *glory* of God described so often in the Old Testament as the visible manifestation of God's presence (see Exod 16:10; 24:16–17, 33:22; 40:34, and dozens of other references).

The incarnation of the Son was a manifestation of God's glory ("the glory of the Lord shone around them," Luke 2:9; "the Word became flesh and dwelt among us, and we have seen His glory, glory as of the only Son from the Father, full of grace and truth," John 1:14). When we recognize this, it is easy to see how the choice of the word "star" was so appropriate to describe just such a supernatural and visible token seen only by a selected number (the shepherds and the Magi). No wonder that "when they saw the star, they rejoiced exceedingly with great joy" (Matt 2:10).

It is that glory which the aged Simeon discerned as he held that baby in his arms ("glory to Your people Israel," Luke 2:32). It is that glory that shone through the earthly tabernacle of Jesus' body on the mountain of transfiguration ("He received honor and glory from God the Father," 2 Pet 1:17). It is that glory concerning which He prayed in His High Priestly prayer ("to see My glory that You have given Me," John 17:5, 22, 24). It is that glory with which He shall come in great power ("When the Son of Man comes in His glory," Matt 25:31).

The Jewish people refer to the glory of God as the *Shekinah*, a later Hebrew word that has as its root idea the concept of "dwelling." Yes, it was the supernatural Shekinah which inspired the Magi and directed their steps to the young Messiah so many years ago. May we also follow that "glory of God in the face of Jesus Christ" (2 Cor 4:6) and go forth to "declare His glory among the nations" (Ps 96:3).

As we have seen from a close reading of Matthew 2, there is indeed a "mythology of the Magi" that embodies some traditional but questionable ideas about these men. There is also, however, some marvelous theology that is not mythology for us to see and to learn in their visit to Jerusalem and Bethlehem so long ago. We just need to look at the passage through the lens of the Hebrew culture to see their real significance.

———▼———

O Lord, like that great multitude in the Apocalypse, you have brough me out of great trouble, and washed my robes and made them white in the blood of the Lamb. Now and forever I will be before Your throne and serve You day and night in Your temple! You who sit on the throne will dwell with me and I will never hunger nor thirst again. The sun will not strike me, nor any heat, for the Lamb who is in the midst of the throne will shepherd me and lead me to living fountains of waters. And You, O God will wipe away every tear from my eyes. Amen.

(Adapted from Rev 7:14–17)

CHAPTER 11

A Messiah for the Rest of Us

Today many people are confused by the differing sects and denominations in Christendom. The Jewish community today is also divided into various groups: Orthodox, Conservative, Reform, Reconstructionist, etc. This, however, is not a new situation. During the days of the New Testament, Judaism also was divided into many various sects. Jesus encountered all of these in one way or another in His ministry.

In an earlier chapter, we examined what Josephus wrote about the four main sects of Judaism that existed in the first century. In this chapter, we want to look a little closer at a fifth group that figured prominently among the early followers of the Messiah.

First, let us briefly repeat what we know about the Pharisees, the Sadducees, the Essenes and the Zealots.

The **Pharisees** were the custodians of the oral law. They placed great emphasis on the traditions that were handed down to them through the years. Also, they were concerned with how to observe the law. Many detailed laws were added by them to help them keep the original law. Jesus condemned their man-made regulations as the "tradition of men" (Mark 7:8). These oral teachings later came to be written down and known as the "Talmud," which is still studied today by religious Jews.

The **Sadducees** were not concerned with the oral law but put great emphasis on the written law, the Torah, which comprised the first five books of Moses. They did not believe in angels, spirits, or the resurrection because they claimed such doctrines could not be found in the books of Moses. Jesus answered a hypothetical question from the Sadducees regarding the resurrection in Matthew 22:23–33.

The **Essenes** were ascetics who withdrew to the desert and believed that they were the only chosen ones of God. They were awaiting the final judgment in which their enemies would be destroyed. Many think that the settlement at Qumran and the Dead Sea Scrolls originated with the Essenes. Although the Essenes are not mentioned by name in the New Testament, some scholars believe that John the Baptist may have spent time with them in his "wilderness" period (Luke 1:80).

The **Zealots** were freedom fighters who resisted strongly the Roman occupation and rule. They attacked both Roman soldiers and Jewish collaborators in guerrilla-type manner. Barabbas and the two crucified beside Jesus were probably members of this terrorist band, which might also be called the "I.L.O." or the "Israel Liberation Organization." Simon, one of Jesus' disciples, was a follower of this sect before he followed the Lord Jesus (Luke 6:15). There were many other groups and organizations in the first century, but these were the main ones.

The **People of the Land**, or the "Am ha'aretz," as the Pharisees called them, were the vast majority of Jews who did not affiliate with any of these organized brotherhoods. This group of people might be called the common folk or the uneducated masses. What did the "people of the land" believe? What was their life like, and most important, how did this group of people respond to the message of Jesus?

The people of the land were the masses in Israel who did not conform to the Pharisaic requirements in their observance of religious duties. The Talmud states that the "people of the land" were those who had not "associated with the wise in order to learn the practice of the oral law" (Talmud Bavli *Pesachim* 49). The attitude of the Pharisees toward the people of the land was one of utmost condemnation. They despised them because they did not follow all the detailed rules that the Pharisees had established. Such an attitude is exemplified by the statement of the great Hillel when he remarked, "No person of the land can be pious" (*Pirke Avot* 2.5).

Probably the strongest condemnation of this group of common people is that found in the words of Rabbi Eleazar who said, "It is lawful to stab a person of the land on a day of atonement that falls on a Sabbath." Said his disciples, "You mean to slaughter him?" "No," he replied, "slaughtering requires a benediction, stabbing does not" (*Pesachim* 49b). Though this may be an overstatement on the part of Rabbi Eleazar, it does indicate the disdain with which the Pharisees viewed the common people. This attitude toward the people of the land helps us to better understand a number of statements in the Gospels and also provides a fascinating background to the Messianic message of Jesus.

One of the strongest reasons for the Pharisees' condemnation of the Lord Jesus was that He was "a friend of tax collectors and sinners" (Matt 11:19; Luke 7:34). The word "sinners" refers to the people who did not observe the law in all of its ceremonial details. Jesus ate with these "sinners" and was condemned for it (Matt 9:11; Mark 2:16, Luke 5:30; 15:2). It was very interesting that in a Pharisee's house a woman who was a "sinner" came to Him. This woman washed the feet of Jesus with her tears, and a Pharisee who was present condemned Jesus for associating with her (Luke 7:36–39).

As a matter of fact, Jesus Himself was considered as one of the "sinners." The Pharisees referred to Him in this way in John 9:16 when they questioned, "How can a man who is a sinner do such signs?" Jesus must have angered the so-called righteous ones of His generation when He boldly declared: "For I came not to call the righteous, but sinners" (Matt 9:13). In other words, He was saying, "I came not to call the Pharisees who are rejecting Me, but I came to call the common people, for they are receiving Me."

In Mark 12:37, after Jesus claimed to be the Messiah, we read that "the common people heard him gladly" (KJV) or "the great throng heard him gladly" (ESV). By contrast, the sophisticated group of Pharisees and Sadducees strongly rejected Him as not being worthy of their consideration. In John 7, following Jesus' teaching at the Feast of Tabernacles, there was a discussion about whether or not He was the Messiah. There were many people who believed that He was the promised Prophet and the Christ (John 7:40–44). When news of this came to the Pharisees, they asked why this man had not been brought in by the officers to be judged. "The Pharisees answered them, "Have you also been deceived? Have any of the authorities or the Pharisees believed in Him? But this crowd that does not know the law is accursed" (John 7:47–49). The Pharisees were referring to the accursed "people of the land," who in their opinion did not keep the law.

In spite of all this condemnation by the religious leaders, the people of the land responded positively to Jesus more than any other group. Why did they respond positively when most of the religiously trained did not? Perhaps it was because they had not been blinded by tradition. They did not hold to the man-made "oral law" which controlled the thinking of the Pharisees. They were often simply believers in the God of Israel and the Scriptures. The sad thing is that many of the common people had more spiritual perception than the educated ones.

One of the most fascinating statements of our Lord Jesus that confirmed His Messiahship was His answer to John the Baptist when John had serious doubts about Him. In Matthew 11:3, John's disciples asked Him, "Are you the one who is to come, or shall we look for another?" The answer that Jesus gave to them embodied a number of signs by which they would know that the Messiah had come. "And Jesus answered them, 'Go and tell John what you hear and see: the blind receive their sight and the lame walk, lepers are cleansed and the deaf hear, and the dead are raised up, and the poor have good news preached to them. And blessed is the one who is not offended by Me'" (Matt 11:4–5).

This was something new in the history of Jewish religious instruction. No one had ever taken so much interest in the poor. They had been the despised, the rejected, the ignoramuses. Here was one, however, who not only performed miracles, but had good news for the people who were despised. Many of the original believers in Jesus came from this large group of the "people of the land."

One is struck by statements in the Gospels about the large number of people who were following Jesus in Galilee but who seemed to have disappeared by the last week of His life. Certainly, there were many who followed because they had their stomachs filled. There were others, such as the Zealots, who followed Him because they expected a Messianic conqueror to defeat the Romans. When He proved not to be that kind of Messiah, they also drifted away. However, there were many who did want to follow Him. Yet, the leaders, the policymakers, and those who engineered His arrest and crucifixion at the hands of the Romans were not from this group of common people.

Following the death, resurrection and ascension of the Lord, the Spirit of God came at Pentecost. Peter preached the good news that the Scriptures had been fulfilled in the things that had happened to Jesus, and thousands were saved. It is interesting to note that the wealthier priests and Sadducees also despised these early followers of Jesus. After they examined the apostles before the Sanhedrin, this was their reaction: "Now when they saw the boldness of Peter and John, and perceived that they were uneducated, common men, they were astonished. And they recognized that they had been with Jesus" (Acts 4:13). The words "unlearned and ignorant" that were used in the old King James Version of this verse may leave a wrong impression to the modern reader. The words are not necessarily intended to be insults but were technical terms that refer to those who had not received the approved religious training of the religious leaders. The statement was not to condemn the intellectual capacities of Peter and John but to demean them because they were not formally trained in the recognized rabbinic schools. Yet, even though untrained and not particular about the details of keeping the oral law, Peter, John and others of the people of the land had the spiritual perception to see in the Lord Jesus what the blind eyes of the religious leaders were unable to see. This Messiah was the One who was the friend of sinners (Matt 11:19). He was the One who preached the good news to the poor, and thus those people were the ones who gladly heard Him.

Paul, an educated Pharisee whose eyes were opened by the grace of God, recognized that it was not his education and social attainment that earned him any favor with God. He states it very clearly in 1 Corinthians 1:26–29: "For consider your calling, brothers: not many of you were wise according to worldly standards, not many were powerful, not many were of noble birth. But God chose what is foolish in the world to shame the wise; God chose what is weak in the world to shame the strong; God chose what is low and despised in the world, even things that are not, to bring to nothing things that are, so that no human being might boast in the presence of God."

Queen Victoria, the nineteenth-century British monarch, apparently was a sincere believer in the Lord Jesus Christ. She is reported to have said once that she "had been saved by an M." When asked what she meant, she replied, "How thankful I am that the verse says 'not *many* of noble birth are called' rather than 'not *any* of noble birth are called.'"

There is no particular virtue in being ignorant. That is not the point of this truth that we have seen about the "people of the land." What is significant, however, is that educational attainments like those of the Pharisees and Sadducees did not qualify them to see the Messiah. Their education in man-made traditions had actually hindered them from perceiving and recognizing the truth. Often the simple people, whose minds and hearts had not been cluttered by human wisdom, were able to perceive the Lord Jesus as the Messiah of Israel when others may have despised His message of humility and repentance.

Jesus today still does not "call the righteous but sinners to repentance" (Luke 5:32). His invitation to be saved is not to those who, like the proud Pharisee, brag about their self-righteousness. His salvation is for those who, like the publican, cry out "God have mercy on me the sinner" (Luke 18:13).

Whether you are Jewish or Gentile, the question is the same. Have you bowed in humble acknowledgement that you are a sinner in need of salvation and the forgiveness which Jesus offers? As long as you pride yourself in your wisdom, your knowledge, and your intellectual and social achievements, Jesus will have no attraction for you. In contrast, if you see yourself the way the blind man saw himself, you qualify for the salvation that Jesus has to offer. After having his sight restored, he was questioned thoroughly by the Pharisees. They questioned the reality of the recovered man's experience because the one he claimed to perform the miracle was, in their eyes, a sinner. One could even say that they despised Jesus as being part of "the people of the land." The newly sighted man answered their attacks by saying, "Whether he is a sinner I do not know. One thing I do know, that though I was blind, now I see" (John 9:25). The blind man had received physical sight and could now see spiritually as well. The Pharisees, though they had physical sight, remained in their spiritual blindness.

How long will you remain in your blindness, my friend? Will you acknowledge that spiritual blindness and come to the only One who can shine upon your dark eyes and heart and give you the light of salvation?

O Lord, Your righteousness has been given to the King, Your Son, our Messiah. He will judge Your people with righteousness, and He will bring justice to the poor of the people. In His days the righteous will flourish, and there will be an abundance of peace until the moon is no more. He will have dominion also from sea to sea, and from the River to the ends of the earth. His name shall endure forever and His name will continue as long as the sun. All will be blessed in Him, and all nations will call Him blessed. Blessed be the LORD God, the God of Israel, who alone does wondrous things! And blessed be His glorious name forever! And let the whole earth be filled with His glory. Amen and Amen.

(Adapted from Ps 72:1–19)

CHAPTER 12

A Son of God

W as there anything really special about Jesus being the Son of God? It is pretty hard to dispute the fact that He referred to Himself by that title and His followers even more so (more on that later). But isn't it true that the New Testament calls each one who believes in Jesus a "son of God?" Yes, it is true, for John 1:12 says: "But as many as received Him, to them He gave authority to become the sons of God, even to those who believe on His name." How does the fact that Jesus is the Son of God differ from my being a son of God (apart from the capital letter of the first word)? Was "Son of God" a title that clearly expressed His deity, or do we Christians read more into it than the Bible intended? The only real way to answer these questions is to recognize how the initial hearers and readers of the Christian message understood that title when they first encountered it.

Who were those first hearers/readers? Well, on the very basic level, they could surely be classified as either Gentiles or Jews. Each of those classes of people already had the concept of a "son of God" in their own first century linguistic and cultural background. What ideas would come to their minds when they heard it used by or about Jesus? Also, did Jesus alter, change or amplify the conceptions of Divine sonship current in His own day? And lastly, did the apostles change Jesus' message and create a Divine

Being out of a simple human Galilean peasant who also was a preacher?

The only way to answer these questions is to look at the concept of the "Son of God" in Paganism, then in Judaism, and finally in the New Testament.

The Pagan Conception of the Son of God

Oscar Cullmann, in his excellent book, *The Christology of the New Testament* (Westminster Press, 1963), summarizes well how the phrase "son of God" was used in the "Orient and in Hellenism" during the period of the New Testament. Following is a summary of his conclusions. Evidently, ancient Oriental religions, especially in Egypt but also in Babylonia and Assyria, viewed the king as a Divine Being and often referred to him in their literature as a "Son of God." In Greek religions, however, anyone believed to be possessed by some kind of Divine power was called a "son of God." The reputation of these itinerant so-called miracle workers rested solely on their claim to possession of some form of Divine powers.

While these ideas helped to shape the worldview of Gentiles who encountered the claims of Christ, their idea of a "son of God" was rooted deeply in polytheistic thought. Therefore, it would be hard to transform it into the monotheistic message of Jesus and His apostles. The variance, for our understanding, would lie in the different articles used to precede the phrase under consideration. While kings and other holy men in Oriental and Hellenistic thought may have claimed to be individually a Son of God, Jesus claimed and was proclaimed to be *the* Son of God. The uniqueness of *the* Son of God concept as it applies to Jesus goes far beyond the concept of *a* son of God in Oriental and Hellenistic Gentile thought.

Cullmann concludes, therefore, that the Old Testament or Jewish concept of "Son of God" should be considered a more likely point of contact for the Christian title. While Gentile hearers of the Gospel message would be familiar with the concept of a "Son of God" with some Divine connection, Jesus' message of being the only "Son of God" would have challenged them with a tone of finality unknown in pagan thought.

Son of God in Judaism

The phase "son of God" is used in four ways in the Old Testament Scriptures. First, the entire group known as Israel is called collectively by this title. See, for example, Exodus 4:22–23: "Then you shall say to Pharaoh, 'Thus says the LORD, Israel is my firstborn son, and I say to you, "Let my Son go that he may serve me."'" Also, in Hosea 11:1, Yahweh says, "When Israel was a child, I loved him, and out of Egypt I called my son." In these texts, the title expresses the idea that God has chosen this people for a special mission, that this people owes Him absolute obedience, and also that this people have partaken of the special relationship with Yahweh.

Second, kings also bear this title. In the Davidic Covenant God says about any one of David's royal descendants, "I will be his father, and he shall be my son" (2 Samuel 7:14). The king too is a "son" as one chosen and commissioned by God. It is easy to see how New Testament writers saw this and other passages as referring ultimately to Jesus. Compare Psalm 2:7: "I will tell of the decree: The LORD said to me, 'You are my Son; today I have begotten you'" with its application to Jesus in Hebrews 1:5. The king is "a son of God" because the nation is "son of God."

Third, early Biblical Hebrew texts sometimes employ the title "sons of God" to refer to angelic beings. This is undoubtedly

clear in the book of Job (see 1:6; 2:1; and 38:7) as well in the Hebrew texts of Psalm 29:1 and 89:6 (ESV: "heavenly beings").
Many careful interpreters of the Word of God believe that "angelic beings" is also the meaning of the phrase "sons of God" in
Genesis 6:2: "The sons of God saw that the daughters of man
were attractive. And they took as their wives any they chose."

Fourth, the title "son" is sometimes used to refer to the same
person as the Messiah. The son that would be born, according to
the prophetic word in Isaiah 9:6, was to be given Divine titles
because He Himself would be Divine:

> For to us a child is born, to us a son is given; and the gov-
> ernment shall be upon His shoulder, and His name shall be
> called Wonderful Counselor, Mighty God, Everlasting Father,
> Prince of Peace.

Consider also its use in Proverbs 30:4:

> "Who has ascended to heaven and come down? Who has
> gathered the wind in His fists? Who has wrapped up the wa-
> ters in a garment? Who has established all the ends of the
> earth? What is His name, and what is His son's name? Surely
> you know!"

Furthermore, the previously mentioned references to the Israelite
King as God's Son are also applied to the Messiah in the New
Testament.

In conclusion, it should again be noted that among the four
different uses of "son of God" in the Old Testament, Israel, a
king, and an angel could all be called *a* son of God, but only the
Messiah could be called *the* Son of God. The Jewish conception
of Son clearly contains the ideas of election, obedience, and
sometimes even a Divine character. It is this last idea that forms

the main background for the use of this phrase in the New Testament. Furthermore, it is this "Divine" idea that informed the mindset of the Jewish people as they were confronted in the first century with the claim that one of their own was *the* Son of God.

Son of God in the New Testament

The title "Son of God" is used in connection with Jesus of Nazareth in three ways in the New Testament Scriptures. Others used the term when addressing Jesus; Jesus used it of Himself; and others wrote extensively about Jesus as the "Son of God."

First, we see *Satan* himself addressing Jesus as "Son of God" in the first two of the temptations: "If you are the Son of God . . ." (Matt 4:3, 6; Luke 4:3, 9). We know that Satan does not question the Sonship of his opponent because he used a Greek construction that implies the "if" clause is true. He chose Jesus' consciousness of being the Son of God as his starting point. As we have previously mentioned, it is significant that Jesus rejects the Hellenistic conception of Divine sonship as being exemplified by miraculous powers. Cullman remarks: "The point of the first two temptations is not whether Jesus believes that God's miraculous power is present in the Son, but whether he will be disobedient to his Father by attempting to use that power apart from the fulfillment of his specific commission as the Son."

Second, Jesus is addressed by *others* as the Son. These "addressors" include Peter ("You are the Christ, the Son of the living God," Matthew 16:16); a centurion at the foot of the cross (Mark 15:39); and even the demons possessing a poor man (Luke 8:28). In addition to Peter's remarkable words, the centurion's and the demons' use of the phrase prompts the observation that demonic fiends and pagans understood more about the Deity of Jesus than many modern "theologians" and cultists. The infamous "Jesus

Seminar" composed of "scholars with an agenda" concluded that all such statements had been invented by later writers. The only inventions in this regard seem rather to be their own faithless conclusions. There were others who addressed Jesus as the Son of God, but the most significant is the ominous observation of the Father Himself, who thundered forth after the Transfiguration experience, "This is my beloved Son, with whom I am well pleased; listen to Him" (Matt 17:5).

The third set of references to Jesus as "Son of God" appears in the Acts and the Epistles. There are so many that the reader need only sample a few representative texts of the dozens that boldly proclaim His Divine Sonship. Perhaps none are as dramatic as Paul's brilliant observation in Romans 1:3–4: "Concerning His Son, who was descended from David according to the flesh and was declared to be the Son of God in power according to the Spirit of holiness by His resurrection from the dead, Jesus Christ our Lord."

The high Pauline conception of Jesus' Divine Sonship is perhaps surpassed only by the Christology of the Epistle to the Hebrews. This anonymous writer is particularly concerned with connecting Jesus' High priesthood with His Sonship. Consider, for example, Hebrews 4:14: "Since then we have a great high priest who has passed through the heavens, Jesus, *the Son of God*, let us hold fast our confession."

Chapter one of this grand writing mentions over and over that the One through whom God spoke in these last days is His "Son" (1:2). This Son expresses the very Divine essence of the Father (1:3), He is higher in rank than angels (1:4–14), and He is addressed directly as "God" in Psalm 45:6 (quoted in Heb 1:8). Hebrews understands "Son of God" as meaning "one with God." To the unbiased reader, Jesus' deity is more powerfully asserted in Hebrews than in any other New Testament writing.

There is one possible exception, however, to that last comment. The Gospel of John is also abundantly clear that Jesus is the Son of God. The title "Son of God" appears more in this book (ten times) than in any other New Testament author. Furthermore, the word "Son" alone is used of Jesus approximately thirty additional times. Let the most familiar verse in the entire Bible begin our brief survey: "For God so loved the world, that He gave His only Son, that whoever believes in Him should not perish but have eternal life" (John 3:16).

But is this "Son" Deity incarnate? We answer that question in two ways: first, by recognizing what Jesus declared and second, by the way His hearers would have understood His words. Jesus' message during the Festival of Hanukkah in Jerusalem, recorded in John 10, is absolutely clear that He viewed Himself as Deity. "I and the Father are one" (John 10:30); and "the Father is in Me and I am in the Father" (John 10:38). These lines recall the statement about the Logos in chapter one. "In the beginning was the Word (*Logos*), and the Word was with God and the Word was God" (John 1:1).

But did His hearers understand Him to be claiming Deity, or, as the Watchtower Society tries to tell us, did He never intend to declare Himself as equal with God? Well, let us let God be true and every man a liar! It is best just to let the Savior speak about this matter.

> The Jews picked up stones again to stone him. Jesus answered them, "I have shown you many good works from the Father; for which of them are you going to stone Me?" The Jews answered Him, "It is not for a good work that we are going to stone you but for blasphemy, because you, being a man, make yourself God" (John 10:31–33).

Later in the passage, it is even clearer that they understood His claim to be the Son of God to be the same as claiming to be fully God. "Do you say of Him Whom the Father consecrated and sent into the world, 'You are blaspheming,' because I said, 'I am the Son of God'?" (John 10:36).

But there is much more. Earlier in the Gospel, while debating with the Jewish leaders, Jesus had experienced their opposition to His claim to be the Son of God. They considered such an idea blasphemous because they clearly understood it to be a claim to Deity. "This was why the Jews were seeking all the more to kill Him, because not only was He breaking the Sabbath, but He was even calling God His own Father, making Himself equal with God" (John 5:18). In the Gospel of John, the title "Son of God" as applied to Jesus means that He embodies the Divine essence of His Father. Nothing less than that conclusion does justice to the texts that we have examined.

Should Jesus receive the same honor and worship that the Father desires? Does His Sonship mean more than that He is just "god-like" in some mystical way? Let the Son affirm finally His thoughts on the matter. "That all may honor the Son, just as they honor the Father. Whoever does not honor the Son does not honor the Father who sent Him" (John 5:23). Can anything be clearer than that?

And how does this relate to the events of the birth of Jesus? Well, let us take it back to some events before His birth! In what we call the Annunciation to Mary, the angel Gabriel predicted: "The Holy Spirit will come upon you, and the power of the Most High will overshadow you, and because of that the holy Child shall be called *the Son of God*" (Luke 1:35). The deity of Jesus was not something that later New Testament writers dreamed up. It was not something that fourth-century theologians imposed on the human Jesus. From the Old Testament prophets through the Annunciation throughout His ministry, Jesus was viewed as sharing in the Deity of His Father. And the title that expressed that more clearly than any other was "the Son of God."

You are worthy, O Yahweh, to receive glory and honor and power, for You created all things, and by Your will they exist and were created. You are worthy, O Messiah Jesus, to take the scroll and to open its seals, for You were slain, and You have redeemed me and my brothers and sisters to God by Your blood out of every tribe and tongue and people and nation. You have also made us kings and priests to our God, and we shall reign on the earth. What a hope! Amen.

(Adapted from Rev 5:9–10)

CHAPTER 13

Epilogue:
Will the Real Messiah Please Stand Up?

W e nearly fell out of our comfortably cushioned synagogue pews when we heard the rabbi's answer to our question! I had accompanied a group of believers from a suburban Detroit church to a conservative synagogue nearby to learn more about Jewish beliefs and customs. We had been given an excellent tour, and now the rabbi was answering some questions. One of our group inquired, "What do Jews believe about the Messiah?" The rabbi's startling answer was: "Well, the Lord has delivered the Jewish people from many trials during our history, and He will deliver us also from the Messiah!" After we recovered from our shock, we inquired further about the meaning of his strange answer. The rabbi then elaborated on the numerous *false Messiahs* that have appeared to Israel over the centuries. These *pseudo-Messiahs* had inflicted much pain on the Jewish community by shattering many unnecessarily raised hopes and aspirations. The damage inflicted by them was so great that many Jews no longer believe in a personal Messiah. The rabbi included himself among those *doubters*.

Over two dozen individuals have claimed to be the Messiah of the house of Israel over the past nineteen hundred years. They represent a wide variety of Jews from many different areas. All of them, however, had one trait in common: they were wrong! Some of the most colorful: (1) Simon ben Kozeba, called *Bar Kochba* by Rabbi Akiba, lead a huge military revolt against the Romans. He died in battle after a long siege of his stronghold, Betar, near Jerusalem. (2) David Alroy announced himself as the Messiah to the Jews of Babylon in AD 1147. He summoned his followers to revolt against the Persian king and then to capture Jerusalem, but he was soon assassinated by his father-in-law. (3) Abraham Abulafia, a learned mystic, announced himself as the Messiah to the Jews of Sicily in 1284. Failing to gain a following among them, he turned to the Christian world to accept his spiritual program for the liberation of Jerusalem from Muslim rule. Having been rebuffed again, he simply disappeared in 1291. (4) Solomon Molko was a Portuguese Marrano (an outward Catholic who secretly practiced Judaism). He traveled from his native home to Italy, Turkey, and Palestine seeking to arouse interest in a joint Jewish/Christian mission to free the Holy Land. After presenting himself as Messiah in Greece in 1530, he was arrested, tried by the Inquisition for lapsing back into Judaism, and burned at the stake. (5) Shabbetai Zvi, the most famous and successful *pseudo-Messiah* in Jewish history, gained thousands of followers all over Europe by 1665. This native of Smyrna, Turkey, apparently suffered from what today is called "bi-polar syndrome" or manic-depression. In one of his manic phases, he boldly demanded from the Turkish sultan that he be allowed to lead the Jewish people back to the Holy Land. The sultan, however, imprisoned Zvi in 1666, and soon thereafter his crushed devotees heard the terrible news that their *Messiah* had actually converted to Islam! He died in exile ten years later.

While never personally declaring himself to be the Messiah, Menachem Mendel Schneerson, Rebbe of the Lubavitcher Hasidim, was hailed by thousands of his followers in the 1980s as the Messiah. Although he never announced publicly that He was the

Messiah, he never publicly told his followers that they were wrong in saying that he was! He died in 1994 and, despite a few die-hard devotees, his Messianic following has practically ceased to exist.

The foregoing *pseudo-Messiahs* are only the most prominent; many others have raised the hopes of many only to dash them in disappointment! Combined with a growing secularism over the past two hundred years, this sad history of Messianic pretenders has had a notable effect on the Messianic views of many Jewish people. Today most Jewish people do not believe in any personal messiah, past, present, or future! Some affirm belief in a future *Messianic age without a Messiah*. Only the small group of Orthodox Jews believes that some day the Messiah will personally arrive. They tenaciously hold to one of thirteen principles laid down by Maimonides in the twelfth century: "I believe with perfect faith in the coming of the Messiah, and though He tarries, I will wait daily for His coming." Many Orthodox, however, are not clear whether such a belief is even essential to Judaism!

Apart from being wrong, each of the *pseudo-Messiahs* had one other factor in common: none of them met the qualifications mentioned in the Hebrew Scriptures that would characterize the Messiah. Most of them ignored these biblical qualifications and based their Messianic claim on so-called miracles, supposed visions, and involved numerical calculations based on *Cabala* (Jewish mysticism). Had the Jewish people measured them by these biblical characteristics, they would not have been deceived. What are these characteristics and, more importantly, has there ever been anyone who measures up to them?

The Tenach (the Hebrew Scriptures) mentions a large number of those Messianic qualifications, and we have spent the major part of this book trying to examine most of them and to respond to the traditional Jewish interpretation of them. As we seek to respond to the Jewish false Messiahs, we will briefly mention a few of them in summary, even at the risk of repeating some things mentioned earlier in the book. The following four "identity markers" are most crucial for helping the sincere inquirer to determine who indeed is the real Messiah.

The Place of His Coming

Micah 5:2 (5:1 in the Hebrew Bible) reads: "But you, O Bethlehem Ephrathah, who are too little to be among the clans of Judah, from you shall come forth for me one who is to be ruler in Israel, whose origin is from of old, from ancient days." This verse simply states that the ruler in Israel will come from Bethlehem Ephrathah in Judah. Although He came out of Bethlehem, He did not have His beginning there, for He is an everlasting person.

God's Word is very precise about this qualification. There were actually two "Bethlehems" in ancient Israel: one in Judah (1 Sam 16:4) and one in Galilee (Josh 19:15). This verse (Mic 5:2) makes it clear, however, that the Bethlehem in Judah is the place from which the Messiah will come. The ancient scribes and rabbis agreed that this Bethlehem was to be the birthplace of the Messiah, and they related this information to Herod the Great when he asked for it (Matt 2:4–6). This birth in Bethlehem, however, does not mean that Messiah is of human origin only, for this verse says His "goings forth have been from of old, from everlasting." The notion that Messiah is nothing more than a gifted man is contradicted by this plain statement declaring His eternal preexistence: He is said to be, literally, "from everlasting." This word conveys an attribute belonging only to the LORD God. "Are You not *from everlasting*, O LORD my God, my Holy One? (Hab 1:12). Even the Talmud and the Rabbinic commentary on Genesis state that the name of Messiah is one of the things that existed before the creation of the world (*Pesahim* 54a; *Genesis Rabbah* 1:4).

So, the **first** characteristic of Messiah is that He will be an eternal being who will come out of Bethlehem in His earthly existence.

The Manner of His Coming

A Divine Being who comes to earth as a human being would have to experience a supernatural birth. The Bible also teaches the Messiah would be born of a virgin—clearly an event involving the miraculous. Isaiah 7:14 states: "Therefore the Lord himself will give you a sign. Behold, the virgin shall conceive and bear a son, and shall call His name Immanuel." The controversy surrounding this verse hinges on the word translated as "virgin." It is the Hebrew word, *almah*, and Jewish writers will often insist that it should be translated *young woman* without implying virginity. They say that the normal Hebrew word for "virgin" is *betoolah*. Although this line of reasoning seems to have a scholarly, authoritative tone to it, a closer examination reveals that "virgin" is a very legitimate translation of *almah* in this verse.

The word *almah* only appears seven times in the Hebrew Bible (Gen 24:43; Exod 2:8; Ps 68:25; Prov 30:19; Song 1:3; 6:8; and Isa 7:14). There is no verse where it can be proved that *almah* designates a young woman who is not a virgin. Especially obvious is its use to describe the virgin, Rebekah, in Genesis 24:43 (compare with Gen 24:16) and the virgin, Miriam, in Exodus 2:8. The use of the word indicates that it refers to a young woman, one of whose characteristics is virginity. This is borne out by the fact that the Septuagint, the Greek translation of the Hebrew Scriptures completed around 200 BC, renders *almah* in Isaiah 7:14 by the undoubted Greek word for virgin, *parthenos*.

Furthermore, the extraordinary nature of this birth is brought out by the word "sign." "Therefore, the Lord himself shall give you a sign. Behold, the virgin shall conceive, and bear a son, and shall call His name Immanuel." A sign in Scripture is something out of the ordinary that attests and confirms a word from God. Most of the eighty occurrences of this word in the Old Testament refer to miraculous signs (e.g. Exod 7:3; Deut 4:34; Isa 20:3). With this in mind, it is appropriate to ask, "What is so miraculous and out of the ordinary for a young woman to conceive and bear a child?" That happens all the time. It would be miraculous, however, if a virgin conceived!

Furthermore, the child born from this miraculous birth is given the name Immanuel. This name is actually made up of three Hebrew words translated literally "with (*im*) us (*manu*) is God (*el*)." This is the meaning of His name which describes His nature. He is "God with us." This was clearly understood by Matthew:

> All this took place to fulfill what the Lord had spoken by the prophet: "Behold, the virgin shall conceive and bear a son, and they shall call His name Immanuel" (which means, God with us) (Matt 1:22–23).

Therefore, the **second** characteristic of the Messiah is that He will have a miraculous birth from a virgin mother and that He will be God in human form.

The Time of His Coming

Calculations purporting to indicate the exact dates of prophetic events have abounded throughout history. Some *pseudo-Messiahs* claimed that the year of their *unveiling* to Israel was determined by secret numerical calculations arrived at through the mysterious practice of gematria, which is the practice of calculating numbers through the corresponding numerical value of a word's letters. For example, the numeric value of the English word "bag" would be 10 since *b* is the second letter of the alphabet, *a* the first, and *g* the seventh.

The Bible knows nothing of this practice. The general time of Messiah's coming, however, is revealed in Daniel 9:24–27. Though there is room for disagreement on the exact details of this prophecy, it is clear that the appearing of *Messiah the Prince* plus His "cutting off" (i.e., His death) would be in the early fourth decade of the first century AD. What is absolutely clear, however, is that Messiah had to come *before* the destruction of the Temple: "And after the sixty-two weeks, an anointed one shall be cut off and shall have nothing. And the people of the prince who is to come shall destroy the city and the sanctuary. Its end shall come with a flood, and to the end there shall be war. Desolations are decreed" (Dan 9:26). The destruction of Jerusalem and of its crown jewel, the Temple, took place in AD 70 at the hands of the Roman general Titus and his legions. What Daniel 9:26 teaches, therefore, is that the Messiah had to come before AD 70.

Therefore, the **third** characteristic of Messiah is that He had to come and be "cut off" before the Temple's destruction in AD 70.

The Purpose of His Coming

If a Jewish person is asked, "What is the purpose of Messiah's coming?" he probably would respond by saying, "To bring peace to the world and to restore the Jewish people from their exile." These themes of universal peace and restoration are mentioned often by the Hebrew prophets. Another prophetic theme, often overlooked, describes an additional purpose of Messiah's coming, namely, to die for the sins of Israel and of all mankind. No greater elaboration of this theme can be found than in Isaiah's fourth "Servant Song" found in Isaiah 52:13–53:12.

This section of Scripture is one of a series depicting the work of "the servant of the Lord" in Isaiah. At times this servant is Israel (e.g., Isa 44:1–2), but at other times the servant is an individual who will restore Israel to the Lord. Consider the key transitional Servant Song which combines both of these ideas:

> And now the LORD says, He who formed Me from the womb to be His servant, *to bring Jacob back to him; and that Israel might be gathered to Him*—for I am honored in the eyes of the LORD, and my God has become my strength—He says: "It is too light a thing that You should be My servant *to raise up the tribes of Jacob and to bring back the preserved of Israel*; I will make You as a light for the nations, that My salvation may reach to the end of the earth." Thus says the LORD, the Redeemer of Israel and His Holy One, to one deeply despised, abhorred by the nation, the servant of rulers: "Kings shall see and arise; princes, and they shall prostrate themselves; because of the LORD, who is faithful, the Holy One of Israel, who has chosen You" (Isa 49:5–7).

In Isaiah 53:4–6 the personification of the *Suffering Servant* reaches a sublime pinnacle.

> "Surely He has borne our griefs and carried our sorrows; yet we esteemed Him stricken, smitten by God, and afflicted. But He was wounded for our transgressions; He was crushed for our iniquities; upon Him was the chastisement that brought us peace, and with His stripes we are healed. All we like sheep have gone astray; we have turned everyone to his own way; and the LORD has laid on Him the iniquity of us all."

The suffering of this servant was vicarious, i.e., for the sins of others. His soul became "an offering for our sin" (Isa 53:10).

The Babylonian Talmud as well as the Aramaic Targums and the ancient rabbinic commentators identified this *Suffering Servant* as Israel's Messiah. Typical of their comments is that of Moshe Kohen ibn Crispin, a fourteenth-century Spanish rabbi.

> This prophecy was delivered by Isaiah at the divine command for the purpose of making known to us something about the nature of the future Messiah, who is to come and deliver Israel . . . in order that if anyone should arise claiming to be himself the Messiah, we may reflect and look to see whether we can observe in him any resemblance to the traits described here: if there is a resemblance, then we may believe that he is the Messiah our Righteous; but if not, we cannot do so (cited in *The Suffering Servant*, eds. Driver and Neubauer [Ktav, 1969], 2:114).

The modern Jewish view of the Servant of Isaiah 53, however, is not that he is the Messiah but that he is a personification of suffering Israel. This interpretation was first introduced ca. 1100 by the great French rabbi, Shlomo Yitzaki, referred to simply as Rashi. Even though most commentators then adopted this novel "Israel" interpretation, there were many who rejected it. As late as the seventeenth-century, Rabbi Naphtali Altschuler wrote: "I am surprised that Rashi and David Kimhi have not, with the Targum, also applied them (vss. 52:13–53:12) to the Messiah" (Driver and Neubauer, 2:319).

However, Isaiah 53 itself refutes the "Israel" interpretation and affirms that the Servant must be an individual who suffers for Israel. In verse 8b, Isaiah states that the Servant was "stricken for the transgression of my people." The problem this raises for the traditional Jewish interpretation of Isaiah 53 can be illustrated by a simple question.

Question: "Who were Isaiah's people?"
Answer: "Israel."
Problem: "How could Israel be stricken for Israel?"

Taking the words of this marvelous chapter in their normal, literal context demands that they describe the substitutionary suffering of an innocent servant on behalf of the sins of Israel.

Therefore, the **fourth** characteristic of the Messiah is that the purpose of His coming is to give His own life as a substitutionary sacrifice for the sins of others so that they might be forgiven. However, in doing this, he would be rejected by His own people.

There are many other prophecies about who Messiah would be and what He would do. He would be preceded by a forerunner (Mal 3:1); He would perform miracles of healing (Isa 35:5–6); He would be crucified (Ps 22:16); He would rise again from the dead (Ps 16:10); and He would ascend to the right hand of Jehovah (Ps 110:1). This is a simple summary of the many prophecies portrayed earlier about His advent.

Is there anyone in Jewish history who meets these qualifications? Certainly not Bar Kochba, or Shabbetai Zvi, or any of the other Messianic impostors, past, present, or future. But there is one individual who fits the composite figure drawn by the Hebrew prophets. His name was Yeshua ben Yosef. We know Him in the West as Jesus of Nazareth. He was born in Bethlehem of a virgin mother (Matt 1:23; 2:1). He appeared publicly in the early years of the fourth decade in the first century (Luke 3:1–2, 21). He was rejected by the greater part of the Jewish nation, died on a Roman cross, but rose again the third day and later ascended to His Father (John 1:11; Matt 27:35; 28:1–20; Acts 1:9). These and dozens of other specific prophecies He fulfilled.

Therefore, we return to the question that serves as the title for this chapter. "Will the real Messiah please stand up?" He has already stood up—over nineteen hundred years ago! He stood up then and said, "Come to me, all who labor and are heavy laden, and I will give you rest" (Matt 11:28). To those who come, He promises:

> I am the bread of life; whoever comes to Me will not hunger, and whoever believes in Me will never thirst. But I said to you that you have seen Me and yet do not believe. All that the Father gives Me will come to Me, and whoever comes to Me I will never cast out (John 6:35–37).

Summary and Conclusion

The evidence for the Messiah from the Hebrew Scriptures can be briefly summarized as follows. He will be a male descendant from the Seed of the Woman who will someday defeat Satan in his conflict with God's creation, man. The genealogy of that Deliverer is to be traced through Shem's descendant, Abraham, and then through his descendants Isaac and Jacob. He will also be a Royal descendant of the tribe of Judah. From the earliest days, it was revealed that He also would gather a following from the non-Jewish peoples as well as from Israel.

In addition to His Kingly role, He will also be both a Prophet like Moses and a Priest like Melchizedek. The psalmists add that He will be called the *Mashiach* or the "anointed one"; that He would be the unique "Son" and that He would suffer for His people but not be abandoned in death but rise to His Father's right hand. He would appear on earth during the first century. In some real but mysterious way, He would be Divine as well as human!

He would be born in Bethlehem by a unique means of conception. He would enter Jerusalem on an animal but would be rejected by His own people. His suffering and death would atone for sins, but He would be raised from the dead and gather a following from Israel and the Gentiles. While there are other indications that He will experience a glorious reign accompanied by world-wide peace, there is reason to conclude that He will suffer *before* those events take place in the future.

Furthermore, in a way that may have seemed strange to those who originally heard and observed Him, the Messiah would be one who would portray the people of Israel corporately. What they were called to do and failed, He would succeed in being and doing. While Israel was called to be a holy *seed*, to be a unique *son*, and to be Yahweh's *servant*, this individual would faithfully portray those very roles in all that they were originally intended to be in the unfaithful people of Israel. Only one individual fits the above description, and that is Jesus of Nazareth. In light of this study, we can understand the enthusiasm of Philip as he shared his discovery with a friend: "Philip found Nathanael and said to him, 'We have found Him of whom Moses in the Law and also the prophets wrote, Jesus of Nazareth, the son of Joseph'" (John 1:45).

And yet, some of the individual prophecies we have studied are admittedly not as clear and distinct as others. Should this cause us doubt because each prophecy does not clearly and without reservation all by itself point to the teacher from Nazareth? Not at all. We can be assured that we are following the right one prophesied by the Old Testament when we see the combined testimony of all of them together. With a measure of humility, we should best conclude with the following well-chosen words on this point by Paton Gloag.

> The real question at issue is not whether some or many of the Messianic prophecies are obscure, but whether we have prophecies sufficiently clear to prove that Jesus is the Messiah. The argument does not rest on this or that prophecy, but on a conjunct view of the whole, on the combination of numerous

prophecies, each of which may in itself be insufficient, but the union of all of which may amount to a proof which is perfectly irresistible. It may be an easy thing to find difficulties and obscurities and vagueness in particular prophecies, but it may be impossible to explain away the whole combination of the prophecies and to destroy their united force. It may be easy to assert that such and such a witness does not *prove* a fact, but it may be impossible to disprove the conjunct testimony of a multitude of witnesses (*The Messianic Prophecies* [T&T Clark, 1879], 145).

O Lord Jesus, my Messiah, great is the mystery of godliness. You were manifested in the flesh; You were justified in the Spirit; You were seen by angels; You were preached among the Gentiles, and believed on in the world, and received up in Glory. May I now reflect that Glory by my grateful and obedient life. Amen.

(Adapted from 1 Tim 3:16)

Further Reading on the Messiah

Baron, David. *Rays of Messiah's Glory: Christ in the Old Testament.* **Wipf & Stock, 2001.** The best popular treatment of the Messianic hope, written by a Hebrew-Christian "giant." Thoroughly familiar with Rabbinic ideas, Baron discusses the major Messianic prophecies, with chapters on some "minor" Messianic evidences as well. Contains excellent treatments of Isaiah 53 and the Messianic title, the "Branch."

Bateman, H. W., D. L. Bock, G. H. Johnston. *Jesus the Messiah.* **Kregel, 2012.** A thorough and scholarly treatment of the "Messianic trajectories" under the rubrics of "Promises of a King," "Expectations of a King," and "Coming of a King."

Beecher, Willis. *The Prophets and the Promise.* **Baker, 1975.** Develops the concept that there is one promise of the Messiah, successively amplified by the individual Messianic prophecies. This "generic" Messianic concept is also developed in the works of Walter Kaiser (e.g., *Toward an Old Testament Theology, Toward Rediscovering the Old Testament,* pp. 101–120 and *The Messiah in the Old Testament*).

Boyarin, Daniel. *The Jewish Gospels: The Story of the Jewish Christ.* **The New Press, 2012.** Talmudic Scholar from UC Berkeley offers convincing evidence from Second Temple Jewish literature that the concepts of both a suffering Messiah and a heavenly and Divine Messiah were held by many pre-Christian Jews.

Briggs, Charles A. *Messianic Prophecy.* **Hendrickson, 1988.** Originally published in 1886, this is a scholarly treatment of the Hebrew concepts of prophecy and the Messiah. Although known for his higher-critical views, Briggs displays an evident belief in predictive prophecy and a firm faith in Jesus as Messianic Lord.

Brown, Michael L. *The Real Kosher Jesus.* **Frontline Press. 2012.** The author of a multiple volume work on Answering Jewish Objections to Jesus takes a more popular yet informed approach about why Jesus is the Messiah, with extensive use of Jewish sources, both modern and Rabbinic.

Cooper, David L. *The Messianic Series.* **7 vols. Biblical Research Society, 1933–62.** This seven-volume series is a thorough and scholarly treatment of the themes of the nature of God, the Messiah, the life of Jesus, and eschatology. Discusses all the problems and issues related to each text. Highly recommended.

Delitzsch, Franz. *The Messianic Prophecies in Historical Succession.* **T&T Clark, 1891.** Originally delivered as lectures to the "Institutum Judaicum," this is the last published work of this great German Old Testament scholar. In 232 pages he accomplishes basically what the title describes. Republished (with Gloag) in The Messiahship of Christ by Klock and Klock in 1983.

Driver, S. R. and Adolph Neubauer. *The Fifty-Third Chapter of Isaiah according to the Jewish Interpreters.* **2 vols. Ktav, 1969.** These German scholars collected the evidence for the interpretation of the Servant Chapters in Isaiah by traditional Rabbinic writers from the Talmudic Period through the Middle Ages.

Fruchtenbaum, Arnold. *Jesus Was a Jew.* **Ariel Ministries, 1981.** Popular treatment of the subject emphasizing Jesus' fulfillment of the prophecies. Also contains other helpful material such as answers to typical Jewish objections and brief testimonies of Jewish believers.

Fruchtenbaum, Arnold. *Messianic Christology.* **Ariel Ministries, 1998.** Excellent treatment of each of the "First Coming" prophecies. Reproduces Hebrew text alongside the English. Interacts well with non-Messianic interpretations. Also contains some very helpful appendixes on subjects related to Messianic issues.

Gloag, Paton J. *The Messianic Prophecies.* **T&T Clark, 1879.** Delivered as the Baird Lectures in 1879, this excellent work emphasizes the evidential value of the prophecies. Has a thorough chapter on Isaiah 53 (pp. 267–313). Republished in The Messiahship of Christ (with Delitzsch) by Klock and Klock in 1983.

Hengstenberg, E. W. *The Christology of the Old Testament.* **Kregel, 1970.** Standard "classic" on the subject for over a century, republished in a one volume abridged, but still a very helpful, edition. Contains thorough discussions of every Messianic text in the framework of a systematic theology approach to the subject.

Kaiser, Walter C. *The Messiah in the Old Testament.* **Zondervan, 1995.** Kaiser brings his exegetical skills and his "generic" approach to Old Testament prophecy to bear on all major Messianic texts. The first and last chapters explain how he applies the "promise" plan of God to the development of the Messianic idea. Probably the best overall and up-to-date treatment of the subject available today.

Klausner, Joseph. *The Messianic Idea in Israel.* **Translated by W. F. Stinespring. Macmillan, 1955.** The most thorough treatment of the development of the Messianic concept in Jewish thought. Traces the idea through its Biblical, Apocryphal, and Talmudic stages. Excellent appendix contrasts the Jewish and Christian views of Messiah.

Lindsey, Hal. *The Promise.* **Harvest House, 1974.** A brief but helpful introduction to the Messianic prophecies. Good to use as a handout to Jewish inquirers.

Meldau, Fred John. *The Prophets Still Speak.* **Friends of Israel, 1988.** Originally titled as "Messiah in Both Testaments," this little "classic" is an excellent summary of the prophecies fulfilled by Jesus of Nazareth.

Riggans, Walter. *Yeshua Ben David.* **MARC, 1995.** Subtitled "Why do Jewish people reject Jesus as their Messiah?" Riggans interacts well with the "Jewish refutationists" and acknowledges their sometimes-valid critiques while defending the Messianic application of the Old Testament prophecies to Jesus.

Rosen, Moishe. *Y'SHUA.* **Moody, 1982.** Brief but insightful treatment of the prophecies with a sensitivity to the rabbinic ideas, with some excellent appendices with useful information.

Rydelnik, Michael. *The Messianic Hope: Is the Hebrew Bible Really Messianic?* **B&H, 2010.** Concerned with both the liberal denial of Messianic prophecy and with a growing evangelical tendency to do the same, Rydelnik offers a scholarly defense of a Messianic reading of these OT texts. Interacting also with traditional rabbinic non-Messianic readings, the author correctly analyzes a crisis in evangelical scholarship.

Rydelnik, Michael and Edwin Blum, eds. *Moody Dictionary of Messianic Prophecy.* Moody Press, 2019. This thorough dictionary, which is more like an encyclopedia, is the "last word" on this subject. I contributed the chapter on Noah's sons.

Sailhamer, John. "The Messiah and the Hebrew Bible." *Journal of the Evangelical Theology* 44 (2001): 5–23. This article is so helpful that it should be expanded into a monograph. It illustrates how the Hebrew Bible was compiled and arranged with a Messianic intention.

Satterthwaite, Philip E., Richard S. Hess, and Gordon J. Wenham. *The Lord's Anointed.* Baker, 1995. The result of a Tyndale House Conference, mostly British evangelicals provide an excellent and scholarly treatment of various Messianic themes and texts.

Van Groningen, Gerard. *Messianic Revelation in the Old Testament.* Eerdmans, 1990. Simply the most thorough treatment of the subject written since Hengstenberg, it excels in its scholarship as well as in its thorough evangelical commitment. Its only deficient area could be in the lack of rabbinic references.

Varner, William. *The Messiah: Revealed, Rejected, Received.* Author House, 2004. Popular treatment of many Messianic texts and themes that also attempts to interact with Jewish objections to the Christian message.

Varner, William. *Passionate about the Passion Week.* Fontes Press, 2020. Focusing on the final days of Jesus and beyond, this book develops how Messianic passages found fulfillment in the suffering, death, and resurrection of Jesus. Takes a fresh approach to some familiar events.

Wright, Christopher. *Knowing Jesus through the Old Testament.* IVP Press, 1992. A study of how Jesus fulfilled the Old Testament hope, particularly exemplified by the treatment of Matthew's Gospel. Discusses broad themes (promise, Son of God, Messiah, Son of Man, Servant) rather than specific chronological texts. Also has an interesting discussion of typology and how it relates to the Messianic question.

CPSIA information can be obtained
at www.ICGtesting.com
Printed in the USA
BVHW031454281021
619998BV00006B/20